# Educational Equality

Harry Brighouse, Kenneth R. Howe and James Tooley

Edited by
Graham Haydon

Key Debates in Educational Policy

continuum

| Coventry City Council | |
|---|---|
| **CEN** | |
| 3 8002 01735 548 0 | |
| Askews | May-2010 |
| 379.26 | £14.99 |
| | |

**Continuum International Publishing Group**

The Tower Building
11 York Road
London SE1 7NX

80 Maiden Lane
Suite 704
New York, NY 10038

www.continuumbooks.com

**British Library Cataloguing-in-Publication Data**
A catalogue record for this book is available from the British Library.

ISBN:   978-1-4411-8483-2 (paperback)

**Library of Congress Cataloging-in-Publication Data**
Educational equality / edited by Graham Haydon.
    p. cm. –(Key debates in educational policy)
ISBN 978–1-4411–8483-2 (pbk.)
1. Educational equalization--United States. 2. Educational equalization--Great Britain. 3. Equality--United States. 4. Equality--Great Britain. I. Haydon, Graham. II. Title. III. Series.
LC213.2.E385 2010
379.2'6--dc22
                                                            2009044097

Typeset by Newgen Imaging Systems Pvt Ltd., Chennai, India
Printed and bound in Great Britain by the MPG Books Group

# Contents

# Series Editor's Preface – Key Debates in Educational Policy

Christopher Winch

IMPACT pamphlets were launched in 1999 as an initiative of the Philosophy of Education Society of Great Britain. Their aim was to bring philosophical perspectives to bear on UK education policy and they have been written by leading general philosophers or philosophers of education. At the time of writing, 18 have been published.

They deal with a variety of issues relating to policy within the field of education. Some have focused on controversial aspects of current government policy such as those by Andrew Davis on assessment, Harry Brighouse on disparities in secondary education, Mary Warnock on changes in provision for pupils with special educational needs and Colin Richards on school inspection. Others, such as those by Michael Luntley on performance-related pay and by Christopher Winch on vocational education and training, have been critical of new policy initiatives. Yet others have been concerned with the organization and content of the school curriculum. These have included pamphlets by Kevin Williams on the teaching of foreign languages, Steve Bramall and John White on Curriculum 2000, David Archard on sex education, Stephen Johnson on thinking skills, Graham Haydon on personal, social and health education, and John Gingell on the visual arts.

The launch of each pamphlet has been accompanied by a symposium for policy makers and others at which issues raised in the pamphlets have been further explored. These have been attended by government ministers, opposition spokespersons, other MPs, representatives from the Qualifications and Curriculum Authority, employers' organizations, trades unions and teachers' professional organizations as well as members of think tanks, academics and journalists.

Some of the original pamphlets have made a lasting impression on the world of education policy and have, in addition, sparked debates in both the policy and academic worlds. They have revealed a hunger for dealing with certain topics in a philosophically oriented way because it has been felt that the original pamphlet initiated a debate in a mode of thinking about educational issues that needs and deserves to be taken a lot further. The Key Debates in Educational Policy series aims to take some of these debates further by selecting from those original IMPACT pamphlets whose influence continues to be keenly felt and either reproducing or expanding them to take account of the most recent developments in the area with which they deal. In addition, each of the original pamphlets receives a lengthy reply by a distinguished figure in the area who takes issue with the main arguments of the original pamphlet. Each of the Key Debates volumes also contains a substantial foreword and/or afterword by an academic with strong interests in the area under discussion, which gives the context and provides extensive commentary on the questions under discussion and the arguments of the original author and his/her respondent.

There are a number of reasons for doing this. Philosophical techniques applied to policy issues can be very powerful tools for clarifying questions and developing arguments based on ethical, aesthetic, political and epistemological positions. Philosophical argumentation is, however, by its nature, controversial and contested. There is rarely, if ever, one side to a philosophical question. The fact that the IMPACT pamphlets have often aroused lively debate and controversy is testament to this. There has been a desire for a more rounded version of the debate to be presented in a format accessible to those who do not have a formal philosophical background but who find philosophical argumentation about educational issues to be useful in developing their own ideas. This series aims to cater for this audience while also presenting rigorous argumentation that can also appeal to a more specialist audience.

It is hoped that each volume in this series will provide an introduction and set the scene to each topic and give the readership a splendid example of philosophical argumentation concerning a complex and important educational issue.

# Introduction

Graham Haydon

## Why discuss educational equality now?

*It has long been recognised that the UK is a highly unequal society in which class background still too often determines life chances.*

*Panel on Fair Access to the Professions Full Report, p. 6*[1]

One measure of equality or inequality is a society's level of social mobility, and among the indicators of that are the factors that influence access to professional careers. That was the specific concern of an expert Panel set up by the UK Cabinet Office in January 2009. Its report, from which the quotation above is taken, was published in July 2009. For anyone with egalitarian leanings, aspects of that report made depressing reading. As judged by access to a range of professions, social mobility had fallen for a generation born in 1970 as compared with a generation born in 1958. The advantages of coming from a relatively affluent home and having parents of professional status – and in particular the advantages of having gone to certain independent schools and certain high-status universities – were increasing rather than diminishing.

From the UK side of the Atlantic, the United States has often been viewed as a less class-conscious society, though at the same time one in which there are great inequalities of wealth and of opportunities in life. On both sides of the Atlantic education is very much bound up with inequalities in life chances. There are important differences: among the most striking is that in the USA there is no equivalent to the great advantages in certain career paths apparently conferred by attendance at independent (private) schools (Full Report p. 18) (in the UK context this means secondary schools, not universities, though it is also the case that the most prestigious universities take their students disproportionately from independent secondary schools). Even in the early years of the twenty-first century, around 70 per cent of judges and barristers attended independent schools (the proportion of the whole population attending independent schools is around 7 per cent). There are also important differences in the legislative context in which schools are run and access to them determined; many of these differences are detailed by Harry Brighouse in this volume.

In the social and political background within which education goes on there are similarities and differences. One regrettable similarity is that both countries have higher levels of child poverty than many similarly developed countries. One difference is that the kinds of policy associated with a welfare state have historically been far more developed in the United Kingdom than in the USA. Thus the United Kingdom has since shortly after the Second

World War benefited (to use what is admittedly a non-neutral description) from what in USA (but not in the United Kingdom) is referred to as 'socialised medicine', while in 2009 what appear from a UK perspective to be quite modest moves in that direction are proving among the most controversial of President Obama's policies.

But while socialist thinking has historically been stronger in the United Kingdom than in the USA, it is well known that from the 1980s onwards there have been strong tendencies of neo-liberal thinking in both countries, which have made a lasting difference to the climate of political thinking, not least concerning education. If the USA is still, in the words of Kenneth Howe in this volume, 'in the shadow of the Reagan Era', the United Kingdom is still in the shadow of the Thatcher Era (these are, of course, essentially the same era, the 1980s). Ideologically the thinking of this era was committed to reining in the powers of government and unleashing the power of the market. Even if this thinking was not always followed through single-mindedly in practice, the policy climate was changed irreversibly – or so it appeared until the closing years of the new century's first decade. Then came the global financial crisis, and the phenomenon of governments that had been committed to staying at arms' length from banking and other businesses, now taking large stakes in, sometimes overall control of, such businesses for the sake of preventing economic meltdown. In the process public attention was drawn as never before to vast inequalities in income displayed in the salaries and bonuses of financiers.

It is a commonplace by now that old alignments and certainties in political and economic thinking have been eroded by the Reagan/Thatcher era and its aftermath, together with the recent crisis. It is widely recognized that the left–right spectrum of political thinking and policy can no longer be applied in any straightforward way (and in any case it never applied in quite the same way on the two sides of the Atlantic). There are doubts over how great the power of government can be and how extensive its responsibilities should be. These doubts apply to education as well as to other areas of public policy (if indeed education *should* be a matter for public policy at all). But in some ways the questions concerning education are among the most difficult.

The relationships between economic inequalities and educational ones are not straightforward.[2] When we see that within the same society some have an annual income in millions and others only in thousands, we can be confident at least in labelling this as inequality in material conditions, even if there is room for debate as to what if anything is wrong with such disparities. In education, what we should be measuring is less clear, unless indeed we resort to almost the same measure – establishing, for instance, correlations between income earned and school attended. But it is one thing to establish statistically that a certain kind of education makes it more likely that those receiving it will become judges or company directors; it is another thing to claim that this kind of education is, without qualification, simply a *better* education than that received by students who end up earning much less. It is one thing to compare the amounts of public money devoted to the education of students receiving different sorts of schooling, but if we find that greater than average resources are devoted *both* to the education of a minority who complete three years of university education *and* to a minority of severely disabled students, any assumption that educational equality involves equal costs to society is immediately called into question.

In both the USA and the United Kingdom a pattern of schooling became established during the twentieth century that for the majority appeared to institutionalize educational equality in at least one respect: namely that in a given area all or nearly all the children of a given age would attend the same school – a common school (Halstead and Haydon, 2008). In the USA this was the neighbourhood school, the predominant form of school provision through much of the century. In the United Kingdom it was the comprehensive school which was developed only in the second half of the century in conscious reaction against an earlier system that had divided children between different schools according to measured ability. In both countries the thinking behind the development of the common school had been at least in part a concern with equality and social justice. And in both countries in the closing decades of the century questions were increasingly raised about whether the common school did or could guarantee educational equality. In the USA there were striking differences in the funding of common schools in different school districts; in the United Kingdom, though differences in school resources (leaving aside the independent schools) were less extreme, league tables comparing the academic results achieved by different schools were interpreted – controversially – as showing that some schools served their students much better than others.[3] In the political and policy discourse of both countries it is increasingly questioned whether the common school is the right model for realizing educational equality, but if it is not, there is far from being any agreement about what should replace it. There is far from being any agreement, indeed, about what would count as educational equality, and about how far public policy should be aiming at it.

Such a situation demands clarity of thinking and carefully reasoned debate. The time could not be more appropriate for a discussion of educational equality among philosophers. Such a discussion should not be entirely at a level of general principle, though it must be partly at that level. It must also be a discussion that takes experience and empirical research into account and can comment from an informed perspective on current policy; and it must be prepared to entertain fundamental challenges to that policy. It would be hard to think of any three writers in the USA and the United Kingdom who are better placed to undertake such a discussion than Harry Brighouse, Kenneth R. Howe and James Tooley.

## The structure of this volume

The nucleus from which this volume developed was a short work by Harry Brighouse on educational equality in the United Kingdom, published by The Philosophy of Education Society of Great Britain (PESGB) in its IMPACT series of policy-related discussions. Harry Brighouse is well known among philosophers of education on both sides of the Atlantic, and unusually within that community has first-hand experience of the school systems in both the United Kingdom and the USA. It therefore made good sense for him to comment on current practice and policy in both the USA and the United Kingdom in the present volume. Given that there are few other philosophers of education, if any, who can match his knowledge of both systems, Brighouse was keen that there should be responses to his paper from both a US-based and a UK-based contributor.

Fully in line with this plan, Kenneth R. Howe in his contribution discusses Brighouse's arguments as they apply to the USA. Howe broadly shares with Brighouse a commitment to educational equality as something that ought to be promoted through govern-ment policy. James Tooley's contribution does not so neatly fit the same pattern, but is arguably all the better for that, in that rather than concentrating on the situation in the United Kingdom (a rather small schooling system compared with that of the USA), he puts the debate in a broader, indeed global, perspective. Tooley was the obvious choice for the UK-based contributor in this volume because he has been a sparring-partner of Brighouse in debates on school choice and privatization, both in seminars and in print,[4] for many years. The present volume allows the long-running debate between Brighouse and Tooley to be taken one step further, and in doing so gives space to a voice that questions whether educational equality should be an object of government policy at all; for Tooley is well known as a critic of state involvement in the planning and running of schools, and a supporter – in practice[5] as well as in theory – of educational markets.

Since Brighouse's essay contains its own introduction, and the pieces by Howe and by Tooley need to be read as responses to it, there is no need here for an editorial summary of the contents of this book. A word is in order, though, about the role of the introductory and concluding editorial comments. Here at the beginning I want to point up two important threads – meritocracy and the benefit of the least advantaged – that run through the three contributions; in the 'Afterword' at the end of this volume I want to take a somewhat more questioning stance towards these two notions.

## Meritocracy

*We want to see a meritocracy where individuals are able to advance on the basis of their talent and effort.*
*Panel on Fair Access to the Professions Summary Report p. 21*

As this quotation from a cross-party panel in the United Kingdom illustrates, the idea of meritocracy has become part of common currency in discourse that is critical of class-based inequalities and in favour of equal opportunities and social mobility. The use of the term in this recent UK report seems very much in line with its use by Harry Brighouse in this volume, when he characterizes one conception of educational equality thus:

> The Meritocratic Conception: An individual's prospects for educational achievement may be a function of that individual's talent and effort, but it should not be influenced by her social class background. (Brighouse, this volume, p. 28)

Although he acknowledges that there can be a more radical conception of educational equality, it is to the meritocratic conception that Brighouse directs most of his attention. Both Howe and Tooley notice that Brighouse does not explicitly say whether he favours the more or the less radical of the two conceptions he mentions; Tooley wonders why not. My own reading on this point, similar to Howe's, is that Brighouse is aware that, within the current climate of discourse and policy, the meritocratic conception is already quite demanding enough, while the radical conception might seem too radical to be taken seriously ('beyond the pale' as Howe puts it [this volume p. 77]). I shall come back in the 'Afterword' to the question of whether we should look to something more radical than the meritocratic conception, and if so, whether this should take the same form as Brighouse's 'radical conception'. For the moment, let's stick with the meritocratic conception, as Brighouse mostly does.

On the meritocratic conception of educational equality, it *is* legitimate for an individual's prospects for educational achievement to be a function of that individual's talent and effort. This conception implicitly acknowledges, of course, that there will be differences in actual educational achievements between individuals; its concern is that the processes that lead to these differences should be fair ones. The meritocratic conception in no way denies that the differences in achievement may be very great indeed; it will legitimate very great differences if the corresponding differences in talent and effort are very great.

Such an account raises difficulties when we recognize that there are some people whose talents and effort are, through no fault of their own, very limited. Leaving aside the point (recognized by both Howe and Tooley) that a person's propensity to exert an effort in education is likely to be influenced by their social class background, we need also to acknowledge that there are disabilities that can severely limit the talent and the capacity for effort of certain individuals. The most obvious case is that of severe learning difficulties; but there are also psychological conditions such as attention deficit hyperactivity disorder (ADHD) that can limit the kind of concentrated and continuing effort that is conducive to learning. Additionally, some severe physical difficulties, that are in no way correlated with intellectual limitations, *may* make it difficult for individuals to maximize the effort they put into education while also coping with everyday life in a society geared to the normally abled (I say *may* advisedly; we all know that there are individuals, such as Stephen Hawking, who exert enormous intellectual effort to great effect while also coping with severe physical problems; we do not know how widely the capacity to make such an effort is distributed).[6]

A strict application, then, of the meritocratic principle as a measure of fairness *could* lead to the conclusion that it is not unfair that certain individuals, because of disabilities innate or acquired (e.g. through accident) end up with extremely limited educational achievements. Given the extent to which educational achievement is correlated in our kinds of society with other advantages in life (which was part of the reason for a concern with educational equality in the first place) we may well wonder whether some other kind of consideration must be given, beyond the meritocratic principle itself, to those who would fare worst under that principle. This is a point recognized by all the contributors to this volume. Should special attention be given to benefiting the least advantaged (who may not be confined to those with disabilities; those, for instance, born into the most deprived or dysfunctional family environments may also be among the least advantaged)? If there should be special attention to benefiting the least advantaged, should we interpret this as part of the demands of a concern with equality or as a separate ethical demand?

## The benefit of the least advantaged

The position of the least advantaged is another thread that runs through the discussion in this volume. Brighouse treats benefiting the least advantaged as a distinct value (a distinct ethical demand, I think we could say), and one that can outweigh the demands of equality, though the latter still weigh strongly. Howe agrees with the importance of benefiting the least advantaged, but he does not think this has to be treated as a distinct value; he suggests interpreting equality in a way that already incorporates attention to the position of the least advantaged. Tooley on the other hand thinks that Brighouse should focus entirely on the education of the least advantaged and stop worrying about equality at all.

Behind this discussion of the relationship between equality and the position of the least advantaged stands the towering figure of John Rawls (mentioned here by Brighouse and Howe, and occurring too in a passage from Brighouse and Swift that Tooley quotes). Such is the influence of Rawls's theory of justice that many philosophers writing on issues of social justice will assume knowledge of it. For any readers new to Rawls, a very brief introduction may be helpful. What I do in the next few paragraphs – which can be skipped by those familiar with Rawls – is to try *very approximately* to follow Rawls in spirit though not in detail so as to show the intuitive appeal in the idea that benefiting the least advantaged is an important element of social justice.[7]

Suppose that a number of people, previously unknown to each other, want to agree in advance on some principles to try to ensure fairness in the arrangements of the society in which they will all be living. They want to do this because they recognize that all sorts of situations may come up in which it is not clear what constitutes fair treatment of individuals by society. If someone comes by a large amount of money through luck, should that person be free to pass on the benefit entirely to their children without any contribution towards the wider good? If a child is born with serious disabilities, should society try to compensate that person in some way? Should society collectively take responsibility for seeing that those in serious need of medical treatment receive such treatment? And so on. If some general principles could be agreed in advance, this might at least give some further basis for approaching specific issues.

If these individuals know in advance what their position in that society will be – if certain people know for instance that they will be healthy and well off and will be unlikely to need material support from others – this could bias their consideration of what principles should regulate the society. So let's imagine instead that these people are behind what Rawls calls a 'veil of ignorance': they do not know what their position will be. This may lead them to be cautious. If there is a possibility for any one of them that they will end up among the least advantaged in the society, they may prefer that society to be regulated by principles that will ensure that those who are worst off – whoever they turn out to be – are at least not any worse off than they have to be. If it is not possible to avoid a situation in which some are worse off than others, then at least – they may be prepared to agree – it is only fair that society should be arranged in such a way as to improve the condition of the worst off so far as possible.

How does this connect with equality? Total equality – if we can make sense of that idea at all – would presumably mean that no one is in a worse position than anyone else. But that does *not* necessarily mean that no one's position could be improved. If there were a society in which everyone barely managed to scratch a living off the land, and no one did any better, there would be equality while everyone had a poor quality of life. In a more developed society, in which disparities in people's conditions of life have opened up, even those who are the worst off in this society may be better off – materially at any rate – than anyone in the simpler society.

There is an argument that the kind of social and economic conditions that allow great disparities in wealth – and all that can be purchased with wealth – to open up are just the kind of conditions that will, in time, improve the conditions of everyone including the worst off. At the time of writing in 2009, leaders of banking and finance can be heard making this kind of argument in favour of their industry being allowed to continue paying enormous bonuses to those who are already earning far more than average incomes. If they are not so well rewarded, then these highly talented highly motivated individuals will no longer use their talents and efforts in the way that will ultimately benefit the whole society, including the worst off.

That is an argument, but that same argument can be turned around. *If* there is some alternative way of arranging society's affairs that would do more for the good of the least advantaged – if it were the case, for instance, that taxing these large incomes very heavily and putting the proceeds directly into benefiting the worst off would in fact do more to improve the conditions of the worst off – *then* how could the disparities be justified? The principles of justice that Rawls defends – with far more sophisticated arguments than I have used here – do have this radical edge. Inequality may be justified by what it does for the conditions of the worst off; but it is *not* justified if there is some alternative by which the worst off would do better.

In this volume, Brighouse, Howe and Tooley do not discuss issues of fairness, equality and justice in such a broad compass. While they all recognize the importance of social and political factors outside of schooling itself, in their discussion here they stick for the most part to the idea of equality in education. As already indicated, they are by no means in agreement about what is desirable *within* schooling, let alone outside it. It is time now to let them speak for themselves. In my 'Afterword', taking up again the same two threads, I shall raise further questions about the desirability both of focusing on meritocracy and of focusing on benefiting the least advantaged.

## Notes

1. From: *Unleashing Aspiration: the Final Report of the Panel on Fair Access to the Professions* July 2009. In references below 'Full Report' refers to this document, at http://www.cabinetoffice.gov.uk/media/227102/fair-access.pdf; and 'Summary Report' refers to *Unleashing Aspiration: Summary and Recommendations of the Full Report* at http://www.cabinetoffice.gov.uk/media/227105/fair-access-summary.pdf. The panel

was set up by the UK government with cross-party and independent membership; its conclusions do not represent government policy.

2. Though within this field *some* relationships do seem evident: for instance, in the United Kingdom the proportion of finance directors of companies who have attended independent schools is similar to that of judges and senior barristers.

3. In the United Kingdom there are some differences in educational policy and legislation between England, Scotland, Wales and Northern Ireland. Since these differences do not affect the arguments of principle in this book, reference has been made for convenience to 'the UK system' throughout.

4. See, for example, Tooley (2003) 'Why Harry Brighouse is nearly right about the privatisation of education', which discusses several works by Brighouse including his *School Choice and Social Justice* (Oxford: Oxford University Press 2000).

5. To describe Tooley as UK-based may be slightly misleading. Shortly before writing his contribution to this volume he had been based in India for two years, promoting the setting up of small non-government schools.

6. The notion of 'effort', used rather glibly in discussions of meritocracy from Michael Young's *The Rise of the Meritocracy* (1958) onwards, stands in need of greater efforts at conceptual clarification than it has yet received. For further discussion on justice in education of people with special needs see Lorella Terzi's *Special Educational Needs* (2010).

7. Rawls' actual theory is *very much* more sophisticated. Among the best introductions that do not ignore the complexities are Brighouse's own in *Justice* (2004) and Kymlicka's in *Contemporary Political Philosophy: An Introduction* (2002).

## References

Brighouse, Harry (2000) *School Choice and Social Justice* (Oxford: Oxford University Press).

—(2004) *Justice* (Cambridge: Polity Press).

Halstead, J. M. and Haydon, G. (eds) (2008) *The Common School and the Comprehensive Ideal* (London: Blackwell).

Kymlicka, W. (2002) *Contemporary Political Philosophy: An Introduction (2nd edition)* (Oxford: Oxford University Press).

Terzi, L. (ed.), Warnock, M. and Norwich, B. (2010) *Special Educational Needs* (London: Continuum).

Tooley, James (2003) 'Why Harry Brighouse Is Nearly Right about the Privatisation of Education', in *Journal of Philosophy of Education* 37, 3.

*Unleashing Aspiration: The Final Report of the Panel on Fair Access to the Professions* (July 2009) at http://www.cabinetoffice.gov.uk/media/227102/fair-access.pdf (accessed on 21 November 2009).

*Unleashing Aspiration: Summary and Recommendations of the full report* (2009) at http://www.cabinetoffice.gov.uk/media/227105/fair-access-summary.pdf (accessed on 21 November 2009).

Young, Michael (1958) *The Rise of the Meritocracy* (London: Penguin).

# Educational Equality and School Reform

**1**

## Harry Brighouse

---

## Chapter Outline

## Introduction

When the IMPACT editorial team approached me in 1999 to write a pamphlet, I knew exactly what I wanted to write about; an essay criticizing the extent to which English schools were able to choose pupils under the new settlement established after the 1988 Education Reform Act. There were many grounds on which to criticize this, but the grounds I chose were that what I called 'the new selective schooling' violated an important principle of educational equality. I still think that much of the philosophy that was in that pamphlet was right, but some of it was wrong, and much of the commentary on policy that was right is now out of date because the UK government has inconsiderately passed two major pieces of legislation on schooling since that time.

So when the IMPACT team recently approached me to ask if the pamphlet could be turned into a book, I felt that it was inappropriate to leave it unrevised. I wanted to get the philosophy right, and also to broaden the policy focus. Soon after its publication, George W. Bush signed into law the *Elementary and Secondary Education Act* of 2001, popularly known as No Child Left Behind Act (or NCLB). NCLB is the first major piece of federal legislation concerning education for two generations, and it pushes the US education system in some of the same directions as the UK system, as well as in some rather different directions. Whereas when I completed the original pamphlet I was anticipating a temporary move to the United Kingdom, and the Philosophy of Education Society of Great Britain (PESGB) wanted direct focus on UK policy, I have now spent almost my entire adult life in the USA; I am much more familiar than I then was with the system of schooling in the USA, and, due to policy changes in the USA, the differences between the systems are less perplexing than they were at that time. So I thought it would now be interesting, and possibly even useful, to provide some analysis of the US system alongside that of the UK system, in the light of a defensible principle of educational equality.

The essay is organized as follows. First I provide a brief account of the main design features of the UK and US educational systems, with two purposes in mind: providing an overview for readers unfamiliar with the system, and identifying the features of each system that appear to be most complicit in the production of educational inequality. Then I provide a brief argument for a principle of educational equality that I believe has a good deal of moral force; but I also provide an account of some of the values that,

I think, constrain how governments should pursue educational equality. I then identify specific features that inhibit educational equality, and discuss reform proposals, which are not, of course, original to me, that would ameliorate equality, without jeopardizing other important values. In brief, although some other values are so important that efforts to achieve educational equality should not jeopardize them, this leaves ample moral space for governments to pursue educational equality aggressively. I have quite deliberately disregarded the preference of some readers to be able to read only about the country they inhabit, or that interests them, mainly because it was more natural for me to write in this, more integrated, way, but also because I think that even if you are interested in just one system, it can be illuminating to learn something from systems with which you are unfamiliar.

The relationship of this essay to the pamphlet I wrote over a decade ago will be uninteresting to anyone sensible enough not to care about my own intellectual and political biography. But for anyone who does care, the earlier pamphlet is probably more like a good-natured yet flawed great aunt, than a parent, to this essay. Suffice to say that, at the time of writing, I think that what I am saying here is all true, and that enough of what I said there is mistaken to need correcting.[1]

## How the education systems contribute to educational inequality

The formal design of the education systems of the USA and the United Kingdom are about as different as could be. I'll describe the US system pre-NCLB first, then describe the changes that NCLB seems to have made. Then I'll describe the UK system, in the course of which I shall draw the relevant contrasts with the US system.

About 60 million children attended school in the USA in 2008, with about 88 per cent attending public (state) schools, the remainder in private schools. Public schools are, for the most part, provided by the 14,000 school districts, and funded by a combination of local, state and federal taxes. The main source of local funding in the vast majority of districts is a real estate tax; states typically top this up, in many cases according to a formula that attempts to offset somewhat the unequal funding intrinsic to the source of the local tax. In some states this additional amount is as low as 20 per cent of funding throughout the state, in others it accounts for more than 60 per cent of funding. The federal government also provides funding through NCLB ($25.3 billion in 2006), and specifically for special education through the Individuals with Disabilities Education Act (IDEA) (nearly $12 billion in 2005). The proportion of both state and federal spending on education has increased over the past 20 years, but gradually, and in a way that has not fundamentally altered the structure of funding or power.

The predominance and source of the local funding combines with residential patterns to ensure that although federal government spending targets need and, in most states, state funding is designed partly to offset inequalities, in the USA a great deal more government money is spent on educating advantaged than disadvantaged children even during the compulsory years. States vary a good deal in how much they spend on education: consider the gap between high spending New York and New Jersey ($14,884 and $14,630 respectively in 2005–06) and low spending Mississippi and Arizona ($7221 and $6472 respectively) (US Census Bureau, Public Education Finances 2006, from table 6). But to some extent this inequality is deceptive; the lower-spending southern states have lower cost of living, and teachers tend not to move between states very much for pay raises. The more striking disparities are within states, between districts which are likely to be competing with each other for the same labour pool. In Wisconsin, the spending gap between the district at the 95th percentile of spending and the district at the 5th percentile was $3500 in 1998, about one third of spending in the higher spending districts; in

Illinois the gap was more than $5000, meaning that the higher spending districts were spending more than twice as much as the lower spending districts (Biddle and Berliner, 1993, p. 5). To close in on what the disparities mean consider Cleveland, Ohio, and one of its suburbs, Pepper Pike. The Orange City Schools in Pepper Pike spent $17,442 per pupil in 2005–06, in an affluent community with a median household income of $133,316 (in the 2000 census) and only 2.6 per cent of children below the poverty line. By contrast the Cleveland schools, serving a community with a median household income $25,928 and with 37.6 per cent of children under 18 below the poverty line (in the 2000 census), spent only $11,073 per pupil (Biddle and Berliner, 1993, p. 5).[2]

State-by-state and district-by-district inequalities of spending are easy to observe and quantify, even once federal funds are counted in. More difficult to quantify are inequalities within districts; but they are not insignificant. Teachers in most larger districts are unionized, and in most union contracts it is districts, rather than schools, that employ teachers. Union contracts usually require that when a post comes vacant it must be posted first only to current district employees, and that qualified teachers have the right of transfer by seniority. At the same time, because of socio-economic residential segregation within districts, schools have different populations. More experienced teachers (who are better compensated and qualified) are therefore likely to concentrate in schools in which working conditions are easier; in particular they are likely to exit schools with relatively high concentrations of high-need pupils.

Does the private sector bear a significant responsibility for educational inequality? It is hard to tell. In contrast with some other countries (the United Kingdom in particular) the greater part of the private sector in the USA is not elite, but provides, at a low cost relative to the public sector, schooling with a spiritual dimension which is unavailable in the public sector. Diocesan Catholic schools in particular have a social mission which results in them having, school by school, a socio-economic mix that much more closely resembles the comprehensive ideal than most public schools, which serve segregated neighbourhoods, can achieve. There *is* an elite sector – the kinds of schools which leading national politicians and businessmen send their children to – but it is small. On the other hand, private schools enjoy, and exercise, a crucial power; the power to refuse admission to and/or expel the most difficult children to deal with. Public schools have no such power; they are the educators of last resort, and there is no clear analysis of exactly how much of a cost this imposes on them relative to private schools.

Children are normally allocated to public schools by neighbourhood; most children, even now after more than 35 years of experimenting with school choice, attend the school that is designated by the school district as the school that children from their neighbourhood attends; and the designated public school is required to admit children within that neighbourhood, and cannot expel any child unless that child persistently breaks rules. This is the neighbourhood schooling model. Since the early 1970s, and especially since the early 1990s, alternatives to neighbourhood schooling have emerged throughout the USA, varying from schemes allowing choice within the public school districts to schemes creating alternative 'choice' schools that are quasi-autonomous (Charter Schools) and, in a few cases, small schemes in which children in need have the choice to opt out of the public schools and into private schools funded by vouchers. It is common, but misleading, to designate these alternative schemes 'school choice' schemes. I will follow this designation, but want to explain why it is misleading. The neighbourhood schooling model was *already* a choice model, because people have choice over which neighbourhood they live in, and for many parents who are relatively advantaged one of the key factors they weigh in making this choice is neighbourhood school quality. In other words, though school choice is not direct, it is nevertheless built into the surrounding institutions.

What is more, whereas in direct school choice systems there is some transparency, and the parents of more advantaged children cannot collude to exclude less advantaged children from the desired school, in the neighbourhood choice model they do exclude less advantaged children by driving up the value of housing within the catchment area boundaries of a 'good' school making attendance unaffordable for less advantaged parents.

Things are different in the United Kingdom. Whereas in the USA, the main loci of power over schooling are the *district*, which hires and allocates teachers and raises most of the funds, and the *State*, which sets regulations and supplements funding, in the United Kingdom the loci are the *central government*, which sets regulation, negotiates salaries, and, effectively, provides almost all the funding, and the *school* itself where school principals are, effectively, chief executive officers.

Since the reforms of the 1980s the formal system for allocating children to schools has been a formal choice system; parents must register choices among schools at both the primary and secondary level, and the schools in question must select which pupils to admit, using transparent and well-publicized criteria. This is a big difference between the US and UK systems, and it also represents a substantial change from the settled system of 1944–88 in the United Kingdom, during which children were allocated to schools mainly according to where they lived.

Some critics of the choice system argue that it represents a form of selective schooling. After the 1944 Education Act most education authorities divided children between academically oriented 'Grammar' schools and vocationally oriented 'Secondary Moderns' at the age of 11 on the basis of their performance of a written intelligence test. From the 1960s this system was phased out almost everywhere, and replaced with the comprehensive secondary schooling that will be more familiar to most non-UK readers, and even to most UK readers under the age of 50. The 11-plus was criticized on many grounds: 11 is too young to predict academic aptitude with any accuracy; the tests used were extremely crude; 75 per cent of children were already labelled 'failures' before their teen years; a society which ensures that its elite will have no contact with those they serve from an early age corrodes social solidarity. But the end of selection gave rise to fears about a loss of academic excellence, and fuelled the anxieties of middle-class parents whose children the 11-plus had heavily favoured.

The charge that choice is selection by the back door at least coincides with the intentions of Kenneth Baker, the architect of the 1988 Act, who has said: 'I would have liked to bring back selection but I would have got into such controversy at an early stage that the other reforms would have been lost.' When asked if he understood that parental choice and the funding formula would kill off comprehensive schools he replies, 'Oh yes. That was deliberate. In order to make changes, you have to come from several points' (Davies, 1999a).

And there is certainly something in the dynamic of the choice system that admits for selection. Writing in 1999, Nick Davies describes the effects of parental choice on two schools in Sheffield:

> There was a surge of anxiety about falling academic standards and a new wave of old-fashioned racial hostility . . . Abbeydale Grange suddenly found itself the scene of a full-blooded white flight . . . the school which had once boasted 2,300 pupils had been abandoned by almost all of the white middle class and was left with fewer than 500 pupils. In the White Highlands, Silverdale was booming . . . Middle class parents fled from Abbeydale Grange and bought their way into Silverdale's catchment area. No poor family from the north-east could afford to make the move. . . . poor children at Abbeydale Grange outnumbered the affluent by more than 3–1. Affluent children at Silverdale outnumbered the poor by the same factor. . . . Neither school is now comprehensive in anything but name. (Davies, 1999b)

An early study by Sharon Gewirtz, Stephen J. Ball and Richard Bowe entitled *Markets, Choice and Equity in Education*[3] helps to articulate how choice facilitated selection and, ultimately, educational inequality. Gewirtz et al. looked at the operation of the 1988 reforms in three overlapping local education markets in London. Their research looked at both the demand side – how parents chose schools – and the supply side – how schools attracted and selected pupils. Data consisted of interviews of parents, interviews of administrators, governors and teachers in the schools, interviews of administrators at the Local Education Authorities (LEAs) involved, and various materials pertaining to school enrolments, choices, school performance indicators and LEA planning meetings.

On the demand side they found a distinct difference, correlating strongly with the social class and educational background, in the ways parents choose. They distinguish three classes of choosers.

- 'Privileged, or skilled' choosers , mostly better educated parents, were better able to understand the public sources of information, including the information offered by the schools themselves. They display 'a marked scepticism about the attempts at impression management involved in the production of school prospectuses and in the organization and choreographing of open evenings and school tours' (Gewirtz et al., 1995, p. 32). They are much more likely to take control of the process of choice, and less likely to allow their children to make the choice themselves. They also display a consistent concern with the social origins of the likely peer group, and an interest in having the child among bright children.
- Semi-skilled choosers are less aware than the skilled choosers of the need to find a good match between the school and their child: as Gewirtz et al. put it, 'the process of school choice is abstract, more a matter of finding the "good" school rather than the "right" one' (Gewirtz et al., 1995, p. 44).
- Finally the least well-educated or 'disconnected' choosers 'almost always began with, and limited themselves to, two [schools]. These would be schools in close physical proximity and part of their social community [whereas the skilled choosers tended to arrive at two schools after a winnowing process]' (Gewirtz et al., 1995, p. 45). The disconnected choosers do not talk about child personality or teaching methods, but focus on 'factors such as facilities, distance, safety, convenience, and locality' (ibid., p. 47).

Gewirtz et al. conclude that the unequal sophistication of parents as choosers in the educational marketplace bodes ill for educational equality. Prima facie we would expect that the worse choosers would get worse schools for their children, and that the privileged children of privileged choosers will tend to congregate together in schools where they can transmit advantages to one another. It should be easier to teach them than the children of the less skilled choosers, and if school budgets are responsive almost exclusively to the age and number of pupils in the school we would expect the per-pupil allocation of effective educational resources to be greater in the schools with more privileged pupils.

Of course, these expectations of inequality could be confounded by unexpected behaviour on the supply side. If, for example, schools all sought a mix of socio-economic class and of ability-levels within the school body, they would be likely to differentiate their kinds of outreach so as to attract all kinds of chooser, and would adjust their admissions policies similarly.

However, Gewirtz et al. found that the supply side responded to the reforms in a way that would lead us to expect inequality. Some school management teams embraced the need to market their school with enthusiasm, others embracing it as a necessary evil in the light of the changed environment. But the incentives were clear, and most schools were pursuing, to a greater or lesser degree, the more desirable pupil base: pupils who are identified as able, well-motivated and middle class, and especially girls and children with South Asian backgrounds. These are the pupils viewed most likely to improve the test scores which will serve as the performance indicators which will be used to attract further desirable applicants in the future. Even management teams deeply committed to some sort of comprehensive ideal were forced by the logic of the market conditions they faced and the content of their ideal into this sort of marketing: a comprehensive school without able pupils and middle-class pupils is not a comprehensive school, but a lower-tier school in a selective system.

The behaviour on the demand and supply sides interact to produce inequality: when schools have discretion over admissions and are not rewarded materially for admitting pupils who are difficult to teach, they will naturally aim for the more easily teachable pupils; and if the parents of the more easily teachable pupils are able to identify the best schools for their children we can expect inequalities to emerge.

That schools aim at the more easily teachable pupils leads to two distinct kinds of cleavage, each of which compromises educational equality. First, children from wealthier and better educated homes tended to concentrate in particular schools while children from lower-income and less-well-educated homes concentrate in others. There was, in other words, the tendency to class segregation illustrated by Nick Davies's report. Second, though, higher-achieving and lower-achieving children were increasingly segregated, as under the grammar school system. Popular schools were able to fill their places from the preferred groups. These schools then needed fewer resources than others because the children were less expensive to teach. The sting in the tail is that the funding formula of the time ensured that these schools have even more effective resources per pupil than the schools which need more. Fixed costs were a much greater part of the school's costs than was recognized by the funding formula, and a school's funding was keyed to the number of pupils it attracts, so that each child brought a fixed marginal sum. So a popular school's marginal income would exceed its marginal costs, allowing it extra effective resources to spend on its already advantaged pupils. But an unpopular school's fixed and marginal costs might well exceed its total income, so that resources would be diverted to the running costs of the school.

The Gewirtz et al. study identifies systemic tendencies, but I want to issue three important cautions. First it is *not* a comparative study between the egalitarianism of the new system and that of the old. The researchers quote Kenneth Clarke's ironic comment that when the comprehensive schools replaced academically selective schools in the 1960s 'selection by mortgage replaced selection by examination and the eleven-plus route was closed for many bright working-class boys and girls' (Gewirtz et al., 1995, pp. 9–10). In the pre-1988 arrangements, even without de jure choice, there was de facto choice as there still is in the USA: wealthier parents could purchase houses in the catchment areas of desired state schools, opt for the private sector, or use their talents at working the system to have their children accepted to their preferred school. Those most advantaged by the new reformed system are precisely the same people who could take best advantage of the previous system. Whether they are more advantaged by the new system than the old is open to question. Second the data was collected from 1991–94, some time after the reforms had been introduced, but before the effects of the reforms were in any way settled. It is possible that some of the phenomena they observed reflected transitional issues. Third, and most importantly, after the Labour Party entered government in 1997, they introduced a series of major reforms, which have diversified the choice system and, in many cases, have significantly mitigated the inegalitarian aspects of the choice system. I shall talk about these in the final section where I propose reforms.

## What is educational equality and why does it matter?

So far I've deployed a vague concept of educational equality, focusing mainly on unequal quality of resources in school. This is a standard focus of debate in the USA, where funding is unequal and correlates not with need but with advantage. In the United Kingdom where, by contrast, funding targets need, but where nevertheless more disadvantaged children perform much less well than advantaged children on any reasonable measure of academic achievement, debate focuses more on the quality of the schools themselves, the character of the peer group the children have in school, and the broader social environment (including the family) influencing learning and upbringing. So it is time to offer, and defend, a more precise conception of educational equality.

We cannot just pick and choose what we care about. The conception of educational equality I develop here matters for moral reasons, and that is why I deploy it in the argument. Other moral reasons sometimes conflict with educational equality; and when they do we have to make moral judgements about how to trade the different values off against one another. I'll elaborate some of those sometimes conflicting values in the next section.

The intuitive case for educational equality rests on an intuition about what it takes for a competition to be fair. Modern industrial societies are structured so that socially produced rewards – income, wealth, status, positions in the occupational structure and the opportunities for self-exploration and fulfilment that come with them – are distributed unequally. Education is a crucial gateway to these rewards; a person's level and kind of educational achievement typically has a major influence on where she will end up in the distribution of those potentially life-enhancing goods. It is unfair, then, if some get a worse education than others because, through no fault of their own, this puts them at a disadvantage in the competition for these unequally distributed goods.

So the intuitive case for educational equality is fairness-based; more specifically, it depends on the idea that, in order to be legitimate, inequalities should result from fair procedures. The dominant understanding of educational equality in contemporary Anglo-American political discourse is meritocratic. Think of the call, in the USA, to 'eliminate the achievement gap' which, if understood strictly, demands that there should be no difference in achievement between children born into lower or higher socio-economic classes.[4] In the United Kingdom successive Secretaries of State for Education have called more explicitly for the elimination of any influence of social class on educational achievement.[5] The best understanding of the principle is what we shall dub the meritocratic conception of educational equality.

> The Meritocratic Conception: An individual's prospects for educational achievement may be a function of that individual's talent and effort, but it should not be influenced by her social class background.

This is very demanding. Given what we know about the influence of social class on achievement, for example, it seems to require that considerably more resources be spent on educating children from lower socio-economic backgrounds than on children from more advantaged backgrounds, and that these resources be spent effectively. In other words, it appears to imply some form of weighted student funding, in which effective spending is inverse to advantage. It also strongly suggests that measures going beyond the education system should be adopted. If it is not known how to educate large numbers of children who are raised in relative poverty to the levels that can be achieved by more advantaged children in the same society, for example, the principle demands the elimination of child poverty.[6] If, as some researchers argue, aspirations to educational achievement are strongly influenced by the educational level of the neighbourhood in which a child is raised, then the principle suggests measures to integrate neighbourhoods by educational level (Ainsworth, 2002).

Demanding as it is, the meritocratic conception of educational equality may nonetheless seem insufficiently egalitarian to some readers. It is concerned to eliminate unfair inequalities in prospects for achievement between children of different class backgrounds but it is entirely silent about inequalities in prospects for achievement between children with different levels of effort and talent. If it is unfair for a child's prospects for achievement to be influenced by her social origins, why is it fair for them to be influenced by her natural talent (which is entirely beyond her control) or level of effort (which is itself heavily influenced by familial and neighbourhood factors)? Thoughts along these lines may exert pressure in the direction of a more complete, and radical, conception of educational equality:

> The Radical Conception: An individual's prospects for educational achievement should be a function neither of that individual's level of natural talent or social class background but only of the effort she applies to education.

After all, no one deserves the talents they were born with, or that those talents, whatever they are, should be socially valued. This radical conception of educational equality may look completely implausible, requiring as it seems to a levelling down of potential achievement to the level that the least talented can achieve. In fact, as I shall argue in the next section, when put in its proper place in educational justice, it does not have this implication. I'll add, as an aside, that despite the apparent demandingness of the radical conception relative to the meritocratic conception, in the USA the education system expends far more resources per pupil on children with disabilities than on children who are socially disadvantaged; in fact, social disadvantage gives a student no claim to extra resources (despite the fact the more advantaged children have more resources spent on them) whereas 'natural' disadvantage does.

Focus for the moment on the meritocratic conception. Standing alone, it permits, although it does not require, considerable inequality of both educational resources and educational achievement, as long as those inequalities do not track social class. For example, it is consistent with concentrating resources on those who have high levels of talent and motivation, with the aim of producing very high levels of achievement for them, while leaving those with lower levels of talent and motivation to fend for themselves with, presumably, low levels of achievement. It would be equally consistent with this conception to concentrate resources on those with very low levels of talent and motivation, in order to produce more equal levels of achievement across the board. The conception simply doesn't tell us. I call it *meritocratic*, because it meshes well with the demands of supporters of meritocracy to reward talent but not class background; we describe it as a conception of educational *equality* because it is closely connected to Rawls's principle of fair equality of opportunity. But, alone, it rejects only one source of inequality. However, as I shall show, when it is put in its proper place, together with other principles it guides us more precisely.

I should mention two objections to the intuitive argument. The first is that we do not, intuitively, think there is anything wrong or unfair about people entering competitions with different levels of ability; intuitively we think that among competitors the most talented, hard working and lucky person should win. Certainly, among competitions that are voluntary to enter. But the labour market is not a voluntary competition; most of us are compelled to enter it, or pay the price of social exclusion and poverty.

The second objection is that society is not a race: there is not 'one Grand Racetrack on which we are all bidden to run' (Lomasky, 1987, pp. 180–1). Of course, society is not a race. But *our* society *is relevantly like* a race. The distribution of the benefits of social cooperation is structured to reward those who do well and penalize those who do badly in competitions they have no feasible alternative to participating in. Different ways of organizing society create different status hierarchies and different reward schedules, which reward different developed talents. Whether someone achieves high status or income depends not just on their own talents and what they do with them, but on the design of the social institutions they are lucky, or unlucky, enough to inhabit. Consider the remarkable incomes that top sports players earn in contemporary developed societies; the talents they have developed command the rewards they do for many contingent reasons for which they can claim no credit, including the entrenchment of the sport at which they excel in the culture of the society, the technology of television which enables them to reach very large audiences, the level of economic development which makes available substantial amounts of discretionary income and time, and low high-end marginal tax rates. However good they are, the exact amount of their income depends on the luck of being better than others. The very good British comedian Mike Winters displayed his understanding of this when he praised his more successful competitors Morecambe and Wise by saying 'It's the kind of act that comes along once in a lifetime; but why did it have to be in my lifetime?'; a perhaps more glaring example concerns Steffi Graf, whose winnings in the 12 months from April 1993–April 1994 were more than double her winnings in April 1992–April 1993 (and her earnings more than quadruple), not because her absolute quality of play improved but because in April 1993 her main rival, Monica Seles, was taken out of the tour by being stabbed by a deranged fan.

Notice two things about the meritocratic conception of educational equality. First, it does not support a principle of equal educational resources, if that principle is understood to mean that the government spends equally on each child in school. As we have said, it seems clearly to require that the government spends more resources on children disadvantaged by their class background than on children advantaged by theirs. Of course, there is another sense in which the government, in spending additional resources on those disadvantaged by class, is attempting to achieve equality of educational resources; it is simply compensating for the inequality of educational resources provided by the family and neighbourhood. But there is no support in this conception for the idea of equal government spending per child in schools. Second, even having put more radical conceptions aside, the barriers to achieving educational equality [on the meritocratic conception] are enormous. Its demands are such that it is hard to see how to achieve it in the USA today, for example, in which child poverty rates are over 20 per cent, in which residential segregation is endemic, where only children raised in households in the upper half of the income profile have secure access to high-quality health care, in which at least 50 per cent of children experience family break-up during their childhood, and in which income inequality is extreme compared with other wealthy countries.

## How *much* does educational equality matter?

Some readers will be tempted to argue that educational equality does not matter, because achieving it would require us to do things that are impermissible. Let's take a simple example; imagine two children, Ron Glum and Barbara Lyon. They are equally naturally talented, but Barbara is raised in a well-functioning and loving family by well-educated parents who spend a lot of time with her, structure her home life in a friendly but disciplined way, and are committed to her education and her long-term development (not just her cognitive development, but also her emotional and moral development). They surround her with books, they put her to bed at a regular and early time each school night, and feed her healthy food in appropriate amounts, discuss her school work with her, and provide her with a range of extracurricular activities that challenge her. Ron, unfortunately, is raised by parents who rarely speak to him, have no interest in his cognitive development, and evince a hostile attitude to the school he attends. What would it take to equalize their prospects for educational success? Almost certainly it would require either neglecting Barbara in a way that would be emotionally damaging, or intervening in Ron's family in a way that would alienate him from his parents. And some children are raised in families much more hostile than Ron's to education and schooling. Removing them, and Barbara, from the family home at an early age and putting them in state-run institutions which carefully treat them completely equally might be the only way to equalize their prospects. Isn't this a decisive argument against meritocratic educational equality?

No. It just does not follow from the fact that in order to achieve X you would have to violate value Y that X doesn't matter. X might matter a lot, just not enough to justify violating value Y. Consider equality and economic growth, and suppose that fully achieving equality would completely undermine economic growth. Suppose, further, the economic growth is very important. Does this mean that equality does not matter? No; it simply means that we should not monomaniacally pursue equality, instead pursuing it only in so far as doing so does not undermine economic growth unacceptably. Of course, economic growth might be so important that we are never justified in pursuing equality at all at the expense of economic growth, but even if that were true it would not mean that equality did not matter, only that we live in a world in which, unfortunately, something more important always prevents us from pursuing it.

Seeing this helps us to refute a common argument against the *radical* conception of educational equality. The radical conception calls for equal prospects for educational achievement between people with different levels of natural talent. But some people are born with considerably less cognitive ability than others, and for some of them there is a very low ceiling on the level of achievement they could reach, regardless of what educational resources were spent on them. You might think that equal educational prospects between them and people with perfectly ordinary levels of talent were impossible, but that seems unlikely; in order to equalize prospects we could severely damage the more ordinary children by, for example, lobotomizing them. To do this would be seriously morally wrong for several reasons, including that children have a right to physical and psychological integrity. Educational equality is not as important as that right, which is why the right presents a barrier to achieving educational equality. But this does not mean that the radical conception fails to pick out a value that should be pursued as far as is permitted by the constraints imposed by other important values.

I've offered no reason here to think that *equality* matters *at all*, and some readers will no doubt think that it doesn't – in which case there is no need to worry about any real world conflict with economic growth.[7] But I *have* offered reasons for thinking that *educational equality* matters. If achieving it fully would involve compromise of other values, we need to know what those values are, whether the reasons for them mattering are strong enough that they should take precedence in any trade-off.

Let's consider three values that are sometimes in conflict with reforms that would advance educational equality. I've chosen the first two because they are frequently used in public, and in scholarly, debate to ground objections to equality-promoting measures; I've chosen the third because, although it is rarely explicitly mentioned, it is sometimes used implicitly, and I think it is a very important value.

## Family values

Few people argue seriously that the USA's school system realizes any kind of ideal of educational equality. But what they do argue is that the measures that would be required to make it more equal would diminish parents' freedom to control their children's education as they see fit. Nathan Glazer's review of a recent book by Jonathan Kozol puts this objection succinctly:

> To be sure, the case for both [racial] integration and equality of expenditure is powerful. But the chief obstacle to achieving these goals does not seem to be the indifference of whites and the non-poor to the education of non-whites and the poor . . . Rather, other values, which are not simply shields for racism, stand in the way: the value of the neighborhood school; the value of local control of education and, above all, the value of freedom from state imposition when it affects matters so personal as the future of one's children. (Glazer, 2005, pp. 12–13)

Glazer hints at a very strong reading of the value of parental freedom; one that actually has a good deal of resonance with, for example, the provision of the Universal Declaration of Human Rights that parents have a 'prior right to choose the kind of education that shall be granted to their children'. If we understand this right as absolute it acts as a very strong constraint on attempts to achieve educational equality. Assume for a moment that some measure of racial integration is needed to achieve democratic competence, and that a child's peers constitute part of her education. On the strong reading parents have a right to demand that their children be educated only with peers of the same race, or in ideologies that are fundamentally undemocratic.

Egalitarians might be tempted to respond by saying that no freedom is really at stake here, but that seems to me to be a mistake. Freedom really *is* restricted; some action or actions are specified which the parent is not free to take. The interesting question is whether she has a *right* to perform the action that she is prevented from taking. Many measures infringe freedom and are none the worse for that. We are barred from bribing trial judges even on behalf of our own children; candidates for political office in most countries are restricted as to how much of their own money they can contribute to their own campaigns; taxation restricts the individual's freedom to use all of her market-earned income as she might like.

Simply saying that some measure restricts someone's freedom does not show that it is wrong. The answer to the question 'Why shouldn't I be allowed to spend my money on trying to save my child from being convicted of a crime she committed?' is that fairness requires the criminal justice system to be insulated from background inequalities of wealth. In this arena, fairness trumps freedom. The answer to the question 'Why shouldn't I be allowed to spend my money buying my child a superior education to that which others get?' is that in order for it to be fair the competition for socially licensed benefits must be similarly insulated. The burden of proof is on the opponent of the measure supporting equality. Mere demonstration that some measure inhibits freedom is insufficient to impugn it. The objector must show that the measure violates some *basic* liberty: some freedom to which we are entitled as a matter of justice.[8] Establishing that we are entitled to a particular freedom requires one to show that it is necessary to some basic human interest in a way that gives others a duty to respect it. So the objection from parental liberty has to shift to offering grounds for the parental liberty, and showing that it can bear the weight that the objection places on it.

The best way of doing this, I think, is to note that parents have a very powerful interest in maintaining the value of the family, and to argue that mechanisms designed to equalize or desegregate violate that interest. How powerful this move is depends on what is included in 'the value of the family'. I don't have the space here to give a full answer, so will just sketch an idea that I have developed much more fully, with my collaborator, Adam Swift, elsewhere (Brighouse and Swift, 2006b, 2009). Our account focuses on the interest parents and children have in being able to have intimate relationships of deep connection with one another. We think that children have a compelling interest in being raised within families, by adults who are charged with overseeing their interests in cognitive, physical, emotional and moral development, and in seeing to their independent interest in having a good childhood. We also, however, believe that most adults have a very powerful interest in being able to play this fiduciary role for some child or children, because being in the kind of relationship that parents typically can be in with children makes a distinctive contribution to their flourishing for which no other relationship can substitute. This justifies allowing parents to spend a good deal of time with their children, and to express partiality towards their children in a range of ways. We think, for example, that reading bedtime stories to one's own children (and not, if one doesn't want to, to other people's) is something one has a right to do, even at some cost to educational equality. Why? If we were prevented from doing *that sort of thing* with our children we would be deprived of the opportunity to create and maintain a valuable familial and loving relationship with them. Similarly, it seems obvious that parents must have distinctive rights to share their values and enthusiasms with their children. They have the right to take their child to their church, and to serve them food that reflects their cultural background, as long as they are not thereby harming their children (e.g. by indoctrinating or poisoning them), and no one else has that right. Both parent and child get something distinctively valuable from being able to share themselves with each other, and for this the parent needs a space of prerogatives with respect to her child.

Does admitting that parents have a very powerful interest in being able to forge and maintain close intimate relationships with their children mean that when parental preferences come into conflict with educational equality, educational equality should always give way? No. Think of racist parents, who resist efforts to desegregate schools because they do not want their children to associate with children of another race. Their preference is clear, but it has no weight here: their ability to maintain an intimate relationship with their child is not undermined by integrating the school classroom. Or think, more controversially, about parents who send their children to expensive elite private schools such as Eton, Winchester or, in the United States, St Andrews or St Albans. Preventing them from purchasing such an advantage for their children would not prevent them from having a successful intimate relationship with their child. (Think about it this way: those schools, when they reject children whose parents cannot pay the tuition, or who do not pass the entrance examination, deny those children the advantages of attending the school, but do not do the wrong of interfering with the relationship between parent and child.)

Giving great weight to family values, as I think we should, has the implication that it would be wrong to force all children into day-care centres for 12 hours a day, 6 days a week, 50 weeks of the year; doing so would simply prevent the establishment and maintenance of intimate parent–child relationships. Similarly, requiring parents to live apart from their school-age children for 10 months of every school year would be wrong, even if it facilitated equality. Whatever we do to promote educational equality must leave sufficient space for the creation and maintenance of valuable familial relationship. But giving great weight to family values does allow considerable space for pursuing educational equality by, for example, prohibiting elite private schools, desegregating schools by race, or socio-economic class, or abolishing academic selection, none of which undermine the ability of families to be successful in realizing the values they, uniquely, can serve.

## Educational excellence

A second value that is often marshalled against efforts to implement educational equality is educational excellence. Think of the debates about the introduction (and maintenance) of comprehensive schooling in the United Kingdom. Prior to the introduction of comprehensive schools, children were sorted (by means of an IQ test) at age 11 into academic grammar schools on the one hand, and vocational secondary modern schools on the other. Only the top 20–30 per cent of performers on the test went to grammar schools which were, naturally, beacons of excellence in some sense. The concentration of those deemed more academically promising and of the teachers with the best qualifications into particular schools created an environment in which high achievement was common. The comprehensive schools movement objected to the early sorting, regarding it as inaccurate and wasteful (not to say cruel), and also objected to the idea that we should concentrate resources only on some children at the expense of others; promoting educational equality was only one impulse, but it was not an insignificant one. Critics of comprehensive schools sometimes object that they are less egalitarian than defenders have claimed, but they also frequently object to what they see as the loss of high-end achievement – excellence.[9]

Sometimes those who cite the value of excellence do so because they regard it as valuable for economic growth; I want to ignore that thought for the moment, because it does not place excellence centre-stage (I shall discuss it in the next subsection). A purer version of the value simply notes that education is valuable because it facilitates the production of excellence: solving complex equations, producing beautiful literature and art, discovering the internal structure of DNA; these are excellent things. If we worry too much about ensuring that the least advantaged get a fair shot at labour market advantage, we jeopardize the production and discovery of excellence. The stock of excellence will be diminished or, at best, not added to. Suppose (contrary to the assumptions of the critics of comprehensive schooling) we discover that abolishing selection at age 11 enhances social mobility (and equality), but at the cost that far fewer students perform at the very highest level. If this were true, than the value of equality would give us a reason to select, and the value of excellence would give us a reason not to.

How important is educational excellence in itself? To give even a rough answer to this we need to ask *why* it is important. The easy answer – because it enables society to generate benefits such as economic growth and technological innovation – assumes that excellence does not matter in itself, and I'm postponing the most plausible version of that view. In fact, the intrinsic value of excellence is more asserted than argued for. Consider John Wilson's suggestion that society should 'allocate [educational] resources to those who can best profit from them' (Wilson, 1991, p. 29). David Cooper similarly says that there is 'a fundamental human concern with the attainment, in whatever field, of excellence; the concern that some should scale the heights' (Cooper, 1980, p. 54). Cooper compares excellence in education with that in athletics and music: 'the prime concern of the lover of music or athletics is not with a general, marginal improvement in the amateur playing of string quartets, or at the times clocked by run-of-the-mill club runners;

but with seeing the highest standards of musicianship maintained and advanced, with seeing great athletes break new barriers' (ibid., p. 55). He goes on to associate himself with the tradition 'of those who see a prime value of education to consist in the transmission and fostering of (certain kinds of) understanding, knowledge, critical appreciation and the like for their own sake' (ibid., p. 57).

I share Cooper's view that one of the central values of education is in transmitting and fostering understanding knowledge and critical appreciation. It would be disingenuous for any academic or educationalist (and I am both) to deny that they value excellence in educational achievement highly, and for its own sake. So I certainly value excellence, and I believe this is not because of some cognitive error, but a response to the real value that it has, even though I can't give much of a justification for valuing it. But the very fact that it is hard to give a reason for valuing it indicates that when it comes into conflict with values that we can give powerful reasons for caring about those other values should normally prevail.

I would like to make a final comment about the excellence objection. Because we are discussing policies, rather than the performance of a particular individual, excellence is a property of a system, and not just of individual performance. So even if excellence were to be weighted heavily in the balance with equality, we would need to have a clearer sense than most of those who are concerned with excellence give us about what it is for a *system* to be excellent.

Consider the following, highly stylized table, comparing four different hypothetical systems:

|  | System one | System two | System three | System four |
|---|---|---|---|---|
| Tony | 165 | 130 | 90 | 108 |
| Sid | 75 | 110 | 90 | 109 |
| Hattie | 90 | 118 | 90 | 110 |
| Total: | 330 | 358 | 270 | 327 |

Does excellence require choosing the system with the highest individual level of achievement? I have only intuitive reactions, which I cannot justify, but that I suspect will be widely shared: My intuition is that system two is more excellent than system one, because it contains considerably more achievement, with considerably less mediocrity. System four, which contains almost as much achievement as system one, with much less mediocrity, also seems more excellent than system one, but less than system two. Systems two and four both seem more excellent than system three, though certainly less equal. System one seems more excellent than system three, but not necessarily better – whether it is all-things-considered better depends on facts that the stylized example does not give us.

Of course, my stylized example does not exhaust the possibilities: policy-makers may be faced with other, harder, choices; and it will never be as clear to them as it is in my example what the effects of their policies will be on the distribution of excellence. But my figures were chosen not to help guide the policy-maker, but to make the point that even if excellence is admitted as a value to be weighed against others when there are conflicts, a good deal more precision is needed about what it is.

## Benefiting the least advantaged

The third value I want to outline is less often appealed to explicitly in public debate than the previous two, but it is sometimes appealed to implicitly. This is the value of benefiting the least advantaged. The basic idea here is that it really matters that social institutions should be designed to benefit those who have the lowest prospects for having a flourishing life. These include some people who have very severe disabilities, and also those who have the lowest incomes and lowest places in the occupational structure and status hierarchies of a society.

The immediate thought of many readers will be that, surely, it is by educating the least advantaged as well as possible that we maximize their benefit, so educational inequality cannot serve them, because it just diverts resources to the more advantaged. But that is not necessarily true, especially in our, highly unequal, world. How might benefiting the least advantaged conflict with educational equality? Whereas within a cohort it is reasonable to see occupational opportunities and opportunities for income and wealth as being zero-sum, the opportunity to live a rewarding and flourishing life is not. The opportunities of the less advantaged for rewarding and flourishing lives might be enhanced by distributing education in ways that violate the meritocratic conception of educational equality. Perhaps wealthy parents could be permitted to buy unfairly unequal educational opportunity for their children, say by paying for them to attend elite private schools, or by paying for extensive private tuition. As a result, *those* children have an unfairly better chance of getting the college places, jobs and status, to which all are aspiring, than other (similarly talented and hard-working) children do. But because parents can invest in their children, they do so, and so the total stock of human capital in society is enhanced; the economy can then harness the productivity gains, due to that enhanced human capital, to the benefit of the less advantaged. Abolishing elite private schools, as the meritocratic principle is likely to require in most circumstances, might thereby harm the less advantaged over time. This is the thought that is hinted at by citing the connection between educational excellence and economic growth that I mentioned when discussing excellence; that excellence may benefit the least advantaged by promoting growth. Or, consider the possibility that the resources needed to combat the powerful campaigns of wealthy parents against egalitarian policies and to prevent them from evading their effects are so great that it would have been better, for the less advantaged, to expend those resources directly on programmes designed to enhance their prospects for flourishing. Adopting these measures to pursue meritocratic educational equality might, then, come into conflict with benefiting the least advantaged.

How important is it to maximize the prospects for flourishing of those whose prospects are least? I take the view that it is very important, certainly more important than ensuring that people who have similar levels of talent and willingness to exert effort face similar prospects for educational success. My reasons for thinking so are basically John Rawls's reasons for advancing his so-called difference principle (to which my principle of benefiting the least advantaged is obviously closely related). The design of social institutions should be justifiable to all who live under them. But there is a deep arbitrariness to the distribution of particular talents and behaviours, and those who lack the talents, or are not well-socialized into the behaviours, that a particular society rewards have much less access to the fruits of social cooperation than others. A reward schedule is justifiable to those who face, unfairly, worse prospects from it, to the extent that it can be shown that someone else would have worse prospects than they do if any other set of social institutions were adopted. Although Rawls himself officially elevates a principle of fair equality of opportunity above the principle of benefiting the least advantaged, I find his reasons for doing so rather weak, and in his final comment on this matter he admitted as much (Rawls, 2001, p. 163 fn 44; cited in Brighouse, 2004, p. 57).

None of the above-mentioned values gives us any reason to reject the value of educational equality. What they give us reason to do is to consider whether particular measures designed to pursue educational equality jeopardize their realization in a way that is unacceptable. Whether a particular measure jeopardizes the realization of some value is fundamentally an empirical matter, one that is often hard to determine. Whether a given level of jeopardy to a value is acceptable or not depends on how important that value is relative to the value with which it conflicts in the circumstances. So we cannot fully evaluate education policy at the bar of educational equality without making some conjectures about the effects of policy on these other values and making judgements about how important they are compared with educational equality. To reiterate, I think that the values of family life and of benefiting the least advantaged are more important than educational equality, but that, once it is detached from the value of benefiting the least advantaged, educational excellence, even on the systematic interpretation I have given it, is less important than educational equality.

## Moving towards educational equality

Both the USA and the United Kingdom experience considerable educational inequality. In both countries reforms that would diminish it without jeopardizing other very important values are available, but different reforms are appropriate to the different contexts. So I shall divide my comments by country. I recommend reading both sections.

But first, the United Kingdom and the USA share two features which impair any school-based efforts to achieve educational equality. They both have very high rates of child poverty compared with other wealthy democracies and they both have high levels of income and wealth inequality compared with some other wealthy democracies. Child poverty matters not because poor children intrinsically cannot learn, but because in wealthy countries with high rates of child poverty poor children tend to grow up in homes which experience high levels of stress and in communities which lack the social resources that support learning, in which criminal and self-destructive behaviours are modelled and in which peer pressures (to which adolescents in particular seem to be extremely susceptible) tend to disvalue learning. High levels of inequality of income tend to exacerbate this effect, because the larger the income gap the easier it is for those with higher income to segregate their social lives from those with lower incomes, and thereby to deprive the children of those with lower incomes of their casual support.

I am surprised how often people seem to be sceptical of this claim. Most people who do well in formal schooling have numerous experiences which, if they reflected on them, they would realize were not enjoyed by those who did not do well out of schooling. For myself, I don't remember my parents helping me with homework as a child, but they did provide me with the space and quiet to do homework, and they emphasized that doing homework well was important; more important than other things I might want, or they might want me, to do. I'm also reasonably confident, having discussed it with them, that if they had thought it would be educationally valuable for me to be helped with homework they would have done so – that is, they made a conscious choice, given their knowledge of me, that I would learn better if they did not help me directly, and, unlike many parents, they had both the time and the educational background, to help me effectively if necessary. But there is a stark example where I got crucial help thanks to their inserting our lives into a network of social advantage. When I was 15 I took an O-Level exam (for American readers this was rather like an AP exam) in mathematics, in two papers on successive days. After the first exam I knew I had done badly, and identified the particular skill I lacked, which would be vital for the next day. My parents suggested that I call a neighbour, who was a professor of aeronautical engineering, and who owed me a favour because every year I provided him with batting practice prior to his annual department cricket match. After two hours of expert coaching, I scored excellently on the second half of the exam. (He, unfortunately, never scored excellently in his cricket match, but I like to think that reflected the quality of his natural talent, rather than that of my coaching.)

My success was due to my access to the network in which the help could be provided; membership of that network depended on living in a small community of people of similar social positions, who made friends with one another and not with people who were both socially, and geographically, distant from them. A child whose neighbours include numerous people with college educations and several who are professors is in a very different situation with respect not only to their access to help, but also the kinds of expectations about how adults conduct their lives, from one only a minority of whose neighbours have graduated from high school. Compare my experience with that of a 9-year-old whose family appears in Annette Lareau's recent, but already classic, ethnography, *Unequal Childhoods*. Wendy Driver, one of the subjects, goes to the dentist with her mother, Debbie, and her brother, Willie. The dentist

> says that Willie has two cavities 'on his permanent teeth' and she tells Debbie 'He needs to brush, especially in the back teeth.' Wendy 'has tooth decay. Let me show you on the X-ray'. Debbie glances at the X-ray and nods. 'The decay is on her temporary teeth, but you are between a rock and a hard spot, because leaving them in will cause potential damage to her permanent teeth . . .' Debbie does not seem anxious or upset at this news of cavities. (Lareau, 2003, p. 216)

The reason for Debbie's lack of anxiety becomes clear in the next exchange:

> Debbie tells Willie, 'You have two cavities that have to be filled.' She tells Wendy, 'You have to have two teeth pulled.' Wendy asks, 'Do I have cavities?' Debbie says, 'No.' (Lareau, 2003, p. 216)

Wendy's mother, in other words, does not equate the term 'tooth decay' with 'cavity' (Lareau, 2003, p. 216). In this particular story there are no consequences; but it is a symptom of the more general disadvantage Wendy faces that when she encounters obstacles in her health and academic life her mother is far less well-equipped than mine were to provide the guidance that enables her to overcome them. Most readers of this book are relatively advantaged, and most have experienced obstacles to success in the way that I have, rather than in the way that Wendy (who is now in her twenties) has. This is not a matter that school-based intervention in highly segmented and unequal societies can readily remedy, and it is a core influence on unequal educational prospects.

The USA and the United Kingdom both have very high rates of child poverty compared with other wealthy countries.[10] And poverty is bound to impede educational equality. Richard Rothstein explains this much-disputed but obvious truth well enough to be worth quoting at length:

> If you send two groups of students to equally high-quality schools, the group with greater socioeconomic disadvantage will necessarily have lower *average* achievement than the more fortunate group.
>
> Why is this so? Because low-income children often have no health insurance and therefore no routine preventive medical and dental care, leading to more school absences as a result of illness. Children in low-income families are more prone to asthma, resulting in more sleeplessness, irritability, and lack of exercise. They experience lower birth weight as well as more lead poisoning and iron-deficiency anemia, each of which leads to diminished cognitive ability and more behavior problems. Their families frequently fall behind in rent and move, so children switch schools more often, losing continuity of instruction.
>
> Poor children are, in general, not read to aloud as often or exposed to complex language and large vocabularies. Their parents have low-wage jobs and are more frequently laid off, causing family stress and more arbitrary discipline. The neighborhoods through which these children walk to school and in which they play have more crime and drugs and fewer adult role models with professional careers. Such children are more often in single-parent families and so get less adult attention. They have fewer cross-country trips, visits to museums and zoos, music or dance lessons, and organized sports leagues to develop their ambition, cultural awareness, and self-confidence.
>
> Each of these disadvantages makes only a small contribution to the achievement gap, but cumulatively, they explain a lot. (Rothstein, 2008)

We know that some schools with low-income populations 'beat the odds' by getting them to perform well on tests and achieve at a level high enough to secure employment and perhaps even college places, but we also know that these schools are extremely rare, and that we do not know *how* they beat the odds. We just do not know of reliable technologies for educating high proportions of high-need students to high levels of achievement.

The conclusion I draw from these observations is that there is something naïve in hoping that educational equality can be fully achieved through measures directed solely at schools. A balanced or, as one movement in the USA calls it, a 'broader and bolder' approach will integrate school reform with efforts to end child poverty, integrate housing patterns by social class and, in the USA, provide reasonably high quality and easily accessible health care coverage for all children (see www.boldapproach.org [accessed on 22 November 2009]).

There is some disagreement about how much, if at all, the current UK government has managed to reduce child poverty. But it has, at least, adopted reduction of child poverty as a central goal, and it has also signalled a commitment to the broader and bolder approach of integrating child and family welfare policy with education policy, not least by reorganizing the government department formerly responsible for education into the Department for Children, Schools and Families (DCSF). As of the time of writing no such commitment has been forthcoming from the US government, although there are signs that President Barack Obama favours such an approach. But what is clear is that the kinds of extra-school measures that would facilitate educational equality are not going to be swiftly enacted, and even if they were their effects are long term. So it is not quixotic to focus on school-oriented measures that would work alone to ameliorate educational inequality, and in harness with other measures to move substantially towards educational equality.

## Admissions

The first issue concerns admissions. In the analysis of the UK school choice system the key problem is not, in fact, choice, but admissions policy. The way that the unequal quality of choosing generates segregated schooling is because schools have a good deal of freedom over whom to admit. In the USA, neighbourhood schools have no freedom over whom to admit, but parents have a great deal of choice; they can simply purchase a house in the catchment area of the school they want their child to attend, and thereby secure admission; this has the collateral effect of influencing house prices to exclude children of parents who cannot afford to buy into the same neighbourhood.

The longest-lived school voucher system in the USA, the Milwaukee Parental Choice Program, deployed a lottery system to prevent schools from doing exactly the kind of cherry-picking that Gewirtz et al. discern in the UK system. This effectively deprives schools of power over who enters the school. It does not constitute a restriction on parental choice; it represents a restriction on the power of schools to choose students, which is a very different matter. And, because markets in schooling are intrinsically highly imperfect, given that in any given market only a few providers can be viable, the lottery helps to restore market conditions by mimicking one of the features of a perfect market, that firms cannot set prices or choose customers.

Since I wrote the earlier version of this essay several secondary schools and one local authority in the United Kingdom have adopted lotteries for admissions, and the government and the Office of the Adjudicator have restricted very considerably the power of schools to select students across the board (except in the very few authorities that retain academic selection at age 11).[11] So I believe that things are moving in the right direction with respect to admissions, if too slowly.

In the major cities achieving heterogeneity in schools would require that children be bussed around the city, since neighbourhoods tend to be class segregated. In some rural areas it may simply be impossible to achieve heterogeneity even with bussing, since the catchment areas may be impracticably large. I suggest that the DCSF, which would be charged with overseeing this requirement, should be allowed to give waivers from the requirement to schools in sparsely populated areas. But the necessity for increased travel expenses in urban and suburban areas troubles me less. Travel expenses are made necessary by two things: parental choice and class-segregated housing. The heterogeneity requirement would create a long-term incentive for city planners to integrate housing, which would be a good thing in itself. But more importantly, if the market in schools is going to produce efficiency benefits, parents should not face unequal barriers to making their choices. One of the reasons Gewirtz et al.'s disconnected choosers seek the closest school is that the opportunity costs of sending their children to a distant school are much higher for them than for the skilled choosers. Parents must bear the costs and inconveniences of sending their children to distant schools, which costs comprise a much greater proportion of disposable income for poor than for wealthy parents. They therefore constitute a greater barrier to those parents, and a serious inequality and market imperfection. Increased travel costs to the LEA are a prerequisite of making the market in schools more efficient.

In the USA, if anything, school populations are more segregated by social class than in the United Kingdom. This is because school district boundaries themselves closely align with the boundaries between wealthier and poorer communities, and because within most districts the main mechanism through which parents exercise choice is through the housing market, a process in which wealthier families have a built-in advantage. I shall postpone discussion of formal school choice to the subsection on 'Choice'; for the moment three things are worth mentioning. First, that increasing the socio-economic heterogeneity of schools is possible through mechanisms other than choice, including catchment area boundary changes, twinning schools and bussing students between them, and, in the longer term, inclusionary zoning policies that require new housing developments to include mixed housing stock. Second, though possible, increasing heterogeneity through these mechanisms is politically difficult; it requires tremendous political will, and will always encounter serious resistance from the families that benefit most from the status quo. Third, and most depressingly, in the US context in particular, heterogeneity within schools is not enough. Non-rural middle and high schools in USA are typically very large: 2,000 to 3,000 students in a high school (which children attend for only four years) is typical in urban and suburban settings. In that environment, within which students typically have a great deal of choice over what classes to take, schools will have socio-economically segregated classrooms unless they make heroic efforts to prevent that outcome, and parents will engage in a cold war over resources within the school, a war in which wealthier and better educated parents are considerably better armed.[12]

## Funding

The second issue concerns school funding. To put the situation simply, to educate students who face the most barriers to achievement to the same level as those who face the fewest barriers takes more money and resources. Higher need students need better teacher:student ratios, they need extended school days and schooling during the summer which replicates the enjoyable and casually educational experiences that upper-middle-class students get from expensive summer camps and spending time with their highly educated families and friendship networks. They need teachers who are at least as good and experienced, if not more so, than the teachers of other students.

The obvious response is to adopt a system of weighted student funding. Rather than granting schools a fixed per-pupil sum, governments should provide funds that are proportional to the need of the student. The Netherlands has long had a publicly funded school choice system that deploys a weighted student funding system; weights are assigned to the characteristics of students' families, so that immigrants bring more funding, as do children from low-income families and of parents who did not complete their compulsory education. Economist Herbert Gintis has proposed a similar system in the context of a school choice system, and a few state governments in the USA now use a weighting formula targeting socio-economic background when supplementing local funding to districts. Here is a simple description of the idea, taken from a manifesto signed by leading education reformers in the USA, most of whom, interestingly, are regarded as conservatives:

> Under WSF, the per-student amount varies with the characteristics of the child. Students with added educational needs receive extra funding based on the costs of meeting those needs. The amount attached to each student is calculated by taking a base amount and adding money determined by a series of 'weights' assigned to various categories of students. These weights could take the form of dollar amounts: an extra $500 for a student in one category, $1,000 for a student in another. Or they could be expressed in proportional terms, with students in a high-need category generating, say, 1.4 or 1.5 times the base level of funding. Either way, the concept is the same: students with higher levels of need receive more 'weight' in the funding system. As a result, the schools they attend end up with more dollars. (Thomas Fordham Institute 2006)

Another variant is proposed in a recent paper from Policy Exchange, a UK think tank associated with the Conservative Party. Rather than identifying a number of qualities that merit weighting, the authors recommend the simpler method of adding £3,000 to the funding for each child who qualifies for free school meals. The simplicity of the scheme makes for ease of implementation, and, more importantly, transparency for the schools and their managers, so that, if £3,000 turns out to be enough, they have a reduced incentive to seek out and prefer more advantaged students. The Policy Exchange proposal, unlike many, does not use eligibility for free and reduced school meals as the sole indicator of disadvantage, but uses a variety of indicators, including, crucially, an index of concentration of disadvantage in the neighbourhoods where the students live (Freedman and Horner, 2008).

Weighted student funding would require a much larger change in the USA, where substantially less public money is spent on educating disadvantaged than on educating more advantaged students, than in the United Kingdom where more is already spent. Exactly how much more is hard to work out, because the funding formulae are opaque, but one UK government minister estimated that schools with high concentrations of high-need children already get about 100 per cent more per student than schools with only relatively advantaged children. This is a good deal more than the 1.4, or 1.5, mentioned in the excerpt from Fund the Child above, and even a 100 per cent premium comes nowhere near to producing educational equality. Working with a dataset from the National Longitudinal Survey of Young Men (NLSYM) and a conception of educational equality consistent with my own, Julian Betts and John Roemer find that in order to equalize the educational prospect of black and white men in the relevant cohort spending on black boys would have had to be *9 times* that on white boys (Betts and Roemer, 1998). Furthermore, there is deep instability in state-level funding formulas, because they are highly sensitive to political shifts, and the resistance of constituencies in high spending school districts. The ideal reform would be one in which the federal government took on more of the burden of funding (which it has already been doing, slowly, over time) and targeted funding directly to schools, almost entirely with the purpose of compensating for disadvantage.

The problem with calculating the right weighting from the egalitarian perspective is that it requires a central planner, but central planners do not know enough about what additional resources are required for educating needy students. Weights are bound to be determined in the context of fiscal and political constraints rather than scientifically, and my guess is that progressive politicians would do well simply to press for the highest weights that are feasible in the circumstances. I do not think there is a scientific alternative; policy decisions are made by politicians who have to be sensitive to what can be done, and are constrained by what it already in place. But Julian Betts has offered a thought-experiment for thinking about the weights, drawing on the experience of energy markets (Betts, 2005). Imagine a school choice system, in which schools have unconstrained choice among applicants. First fund the schools equally on a per-student basis. Then distribute 'trade-able' rights to admit highly advantaged students; and allow schools to auction those rights. Schools would then be forced to figure out how much they valued the money they were spending relative to the highly advantaged children they wanted. We don't know what the outcome would be. At one end of the spectrum you'd have schools with high concentrations of advantage and not much money; at the other end of the spectrum high concentrations of disadvantage and loads of money. It would probably take a few years for administrators to work out what the real costs of disadvantaged children were; but they would have a powerful incentive to work it out. It doesn't take a great deal of imagination to see that in both the USA and the United Kingdom this method would generate very large weights.

## Choice

What is the place of school choice in systems devoted to educational equality? There is a very strong, and regrettable, tendency on the left to see choice as the enemy of equality and therefore to assume that choice should have no place in an egalitarian policy framework. The observation that choice is the enemy of equality is, I should say, true. The purpose of choice in the provision of public services is to trigger competition which is, in turn, supposed to improve performance of the competing units. In order for choice to have the benefits claimed for it with respect to quality it must have the side effect of compromising equality; if it did not then it could not yield the efficiency gains that purportedly justify it.

If choice is going to be used to improve provision of these services it must be because better providers are chosen by more people. Those who choose the worse providers get worse provision. The better and worse providers have to compete. *Over time* this should produce improvement (if markets work as their enthusiasts claim). But *at any given time* there will be better and worse providers – those who have the worse providers are worse off (in one relevant respect) than those who have the better providers.

In fact there are reasons to be sceptical that choice will yield substantial efficiency benefits in schooling. Enthusiasts for school choice tend to overestimate the quality of information that parents have, and to underestimate (or even ignore) the transaction costs consumers face, and the power that producers have in educational markets. They tend to assume, in other words, that markets in schooling can be more perfect than they really can be.

Think first about the quality of information. The UK government goes to great lengths to produce good quality information for parents about the quality of the schools they are choosing among. For over 20 years the government has constructed an elaborate set of league tables comparing schools by looking at the scores of children in various tests at key ages. The states involved in NCLB are, rather slowly, moving in the same direction. But these tables in the UK case include weightings of the significance of different tests which are, at best, counter-intuitive, and understanding the full import of the tables takes more time and education than most parents are willing to give it. Worse, until recently the tables were constructed out of raw scores, so told parents something about the achievement levels of the students, but nothing very much about the quality of the schooling they received. Constructing useful value-added tables is difficult. The government has instituted a scheme that will, in theory, record all relevant data (test/exam results, schools attended and a few other things) concerning every pupil from age 4 to 16. If these data were accurately gathered, they would, in principle, allow for value-added tables. It is worth emphasizing what a massive data-gathering task this is: for example, since we know that socio-economic background is a predictor of outcomes, quite detailed data on the (relatively frequent) movements between income deciles of children's families would be needed. There are serious problems concerning the effects of pupil mobility, and reasonable doubts that the data can be gathered accurately. The UK government has, in fact, adopted value-added measures, but has done so without solving these problems (see www.dfes.gov.uk/performancetables [accessed on 22 November 2009]). Even if these problems are overcome, however, there remain two insuperable difficulties, as Harvey Goldstein explains:

> Schools cannot be summarized by a single value-added score – they are differentially 'effective' for different kinds of pupil and in different subjects.
>
> More seriously, the numbers are smallish so that sampling error gives you very wide uncertainty intervals and this means that for anything between 60 and 80% of schools they cannot be distinguished from the overall average! Some schools do turn up as extreme but will not all do so over time, and it is also very difficult to detect schools that are changing consistently over time. In other words, for most schools there is no statistically valid way that they can be ranked. Even where you do detect an 'outlier' there may be a good reason for this over which the school has little control. (Goldstein, 1997)[13]

On the most optimistic assumptions, value-added tables will help parents avoid (or leap at) the extremes, and not in making discriminations between the vast majority of schools that fall within the normal range.

Nor is it clear that even good value-added tables give many parents relevant information. The *relevant* information parents need is highly peculiar – it is not how good the school is, but how high the probability is that it will be good for *one's own* child. Suppose one knows that one's child is going to be a high achiever in pretty much any school that does not set out to destroy her, and has confidence that all the schools in the local area will be adequate in that sense; one might seek the school in which she has the best chance of having a reasonably sized friendship network, or in which she will have the best chance of avoiding a certain kind of teasing. One might, alternatively, simply want to make sure that she avoids being at school with one or two other particular children. Some of this information can be gleaned through informal means, but much of it is simply not available at all.

Now consider transaction costs. These are also high for parents, and, to make matters worse, they are borne by children. Once a child is in a school she will usually be better off in that school than moving to another, somewhat better, school, because the move is, itself, costly to her educational prospects and her emotional well-being. It takes time and emotional energy to make friends and it is more distracting from one's school work to be making new friendships than to be maintaining existing friendships. It also takes time for a teacher to get to know a child, and to tailor her instruction to that child's needs. One or two transitions during a school career may be fine, but a wise parent concerned with her child's prospects and happiness will avoid imposing on her child the numerous moves that would be needed for consumer choice to have an optimal effect on the quality of producers. Compare this with the now trivial transaction costs involved in frequent changes in one's chosen brand of breakfast cereal.

For this reason and others producers (schools) also have a good deal of market power. Schools must be above a certain size to be viable, so supply is inevitably restricted, and none will be exactly what the consumer wants. Any particular consumer has at most five or six schools that are realistic for them to use. The highly limited supply is a serious market imperfection. It can be diminished or enhanced, of course, by regulation; neighbourhood schooling gives schools more market power than they would have some choice systems, the UK practice of allowing various forms of selection of students by schools gives them even more power.

The case for or against any particular version of choice, then, has to forgo a generalized optimism about the capacity of markets to improve productivity, and must focus specifically on the details of the scheme being proposed or defended, and compare it with those of other schemes that are on the table with respect to some desired goals.

So, after all these negative comments about choice, why do I think it unfortunate that left-wing commentators tend to assume that there should be no choice in the school system? The main reason is simply this. *There is no school system without school choice, and those who oppose school choice typically ignore the massive, and unjust, significance of choice in the pre-existing system.* In the system of neighbourhood schooling that more or less dominated the United Kingdom before 1988 and still predominates in most of the USA, children are allocated to schools in a way that is sensitive to the choices of their parents: the choice about which house to live in. Middle-class and wealthy parents who are unsatisfied with their children's schools have a choice. They can move to the neighbourhood within their district where most of the middle-class and wealthy children go. Or they can move to the suburbs, where their children's school will spend, in the USA, considerably more per pupil than an inner-city school. Thus do schools segregate by class, and neighbourhoods too: the system of neighbourhood public schooling in the USA not only reflects, but also contributes to, the segregation of neighbourhoods. If schools segregate by race, and the school district or districts involved can be implicated by the courts, something can be done. But mere segregation by class is written into the structure of US public schooling. In effect, neighbourhood schooling with local funding, is a huge voucher system, in which the size of the voucher is roughly proportional to the income level of the community in which the child lives, and in which only those who can afford to move house can choose in which school to use the voucher.

Formal school choice schemes do not introduce choice into the way that children are allocated to schools; they redistribute choice. Some formal choice schemes redistribute choice in an even less egalitarian way; for example, several US states have inter-district choice schemes in which children can attend schools in different districts but, usually, only if there is spare capacity after the children from that district have all, already, been admitted; given the superior access to information and transport of upper-middle-class parents they are the only people likely to make use of this choice. But other formal systems of choice, such as those which target vouchers to children from low-income homes, or those which require all parents to register choices, offer to pay for transportation, and limit the ability of schools to select students have real potential for being more egalitarian than the pre-existing *status quo*.

## Accountability

The Conservative legislation of the 1980s in the United Kingdom introduced, gradually, increasing requirements on schools to publish the academic results of students, and from 1997 the government started to gather quite detailed individual-level data on students. There had long been a system of school inspections (modelled on the factory inspections introduced by the Factory Acts in the nineteenth century) but whereas the inspections had previously been designed to identify very bad practices, and to spread good practices, the regime developed in the 1990s increasingly made public fine-grained judgements about the relative performance of schools. A similar movement in the USA lagged several years behind, but gradually became more monomaniacal than the UK system in its focus on how well children performed on tests of basic skills; and the debates around accountability were less sensitive to issues about the reliability and validity of the statistical methods used to measure school performance. In 2002

George W. Bush signed the only significant piece of domestic legislation of his Presidency, the so-called No Child Left Behind Act (NCLB), which introduced moderate accountability requirements, operating through the states.

The accountability systems in both countries are quite complex, and this is not the place to make a comprehensive evaluation of either system, nor to make elaborate suggestions for reform (see Rothstein et al., 2008). For what it is worth, I hold the now (writing in 2009) more-or-less consensus opinion that NCLB was very badly designed and requires dramatic reform; and I also believe that significant reform is needed in the much better designed system in the United Kingdom. But I also believe that some form of accountability is necessary if we expect schools to play a role in reducing educational inequality in a highly unequal society. So I want to discuss two specific issues, both of which are common to the two systems.

The first concerns the requirement, in NCLB, that data be provided on the performance of children from different demographic groups, including those from different ethnic groups, and different socio-economic backgrounds. NCLB requires that schools improve the proportions of students who achieve 'proficiency' in certain basic skills, as measured by tests at different grade levels, rather than requiring that they improve the mean level of performance on some scale.[14] By requiring that data be disaggregated by ethnic group and socio-economic class (something that very few states did beforehand) it highlights the performance of those groups, and creates a pressure for improving their performance. In doing so it has established a counter-pressure to the normal operation of power within a localized system of power over schooling. Local control favours the educated, the wealthy and the articulate; not only because they can segregate themselves into separate districts and get better funding for their children's schools, but because when they are in the same district as less wealthy, educated and articulate parents, they can deploy their schools to get advantages for their kids. Consider the following rather stylized example: a district has two schools, Carter Elementary, with a 25 per cent poverty rate, and Reagan Elementary, with a 90 per cent poverty rate. The (very good) principals of both schools retire and the Superintendent has only one very good, and one mediocre, principal to replace them with. Prior to NCLB what are his incentives? Assigning the very good principal to Carter Elementary keeps the Carter parents satisfied; they are the parents who will lobby hard if their school is assigned a sloppy principal, whereas the Reagan parents will spend much less time talking to the principal and monitoring her performance, and a significant proportion of them lack both the confidence to make complaints and the skills to articulate their complaints effectively if they do. NCLB has changed his incentives: he is under pressure from the state, and the state is under pressure from the Feds, to improve the achievement of the lowest achievers, and one factor in that is likely to be the assignment of an excellent principal to the school with high proportions of low-income children.

The example above, though drawn from an actual experience, is stylized. Without a detailed exploration of the actual decision-making of Superintendents we cannot be sure how they actually respond to the incentives. But Stacy Lee, in her ethnography on the ways that Hmong children negotiate their experience of a mainly white High School in the US Midwest, reports the following:

> Educators who express concern for students of color suggest that the inequality among students is related to the inequality among UHS parents. These educators point to the power of elite parents to control and reproduce elite school culture. Mr. Burns, for example, maintained the UHS is most responsive to students from highly educated families because their parents pressure the school to serve their interests. UHS educators explained that the highly educated parents exert a great deal of influence over the school because they understand and know how to manipulate the unwritten rules that govern schools. These parents know which courses and activities will impress college admissions officers, and they make every effort to ensure their children have advantages. They know about various scholarships and awards and they are invested in helping their

children win them. In short, the highly educated parents possess the entitlement and the type of cultural capital recognized by UHS and by institutions of higher education. Other researchers have identified similar patterns of responding to the demand of powerful parents. Gitlin et al. found 'A concern for white parents quickly becomes a concern for the school because those parents had the economic and social power to make strong demands on teachers and administrator.' (Lee, S., 2005, p. 38)

The concern about developing an accountability system to counteract the inegalitarian effects of local control is specific to the USA; but a more generalizable point is also worth making, which is that educators at every level need good information in order to meet the challenge that the educational egalitarian sets them, and that includes information about how well children are performing at the low end of the achievement spectrum, and about who, exactly, those children are. Any successor of NCLB, and any revision of the accountability system in the United Kingdom should continue to gather individual-level data and ensure that there is good demographic information about low-achievers.

The second issue concerns what in the USA are called the 'bubble kids'. The USA and United Kingdom share the problem, though it arises in different ways. In the USA, because the aim is ensure that more children reach the threshold of proficiency, there are very clear incentives to focus resources on children who are close either side of that threshold. In the United Kingdom, schools are ranked by the proportions of children who attain 5 GCSE's at grades A–C at age 16; again, there is a clear incentive both to focus resources on those who are close to the borderline of a C, but also to game the system by guiding children to GCSE's that are easier for them to get C's in.

Not only are the incentives clear, but there is pretty good evidence that the phenomenon at least sometimes occurs. Take the following story:

The principal of Earle B. Wood Middle School in Rockville gathered teachers and handed out a list of all the black, Hispanic, special-education and limited-English-speaking students who would take the Maryland School Assessment, the measure of success or failure under the federal No Child Left Behind mandate.

Principal Renee Foose told teachers to cross off the names of students who had virtually no chance of passing and those certain to pass. Those who remained, children on the cusp between success and failure, would receive 45 minutes of intensive test preparation four days a week, until further notice. (de Vise, 2007)[15]

My interest here is in what the educational egalitarian should make of the phenomenon. Critics object to the incentive to focus on the 'bubble kids' for a number of reasons. Some are specific to the character of the tests involved. For example, training a child to do a little better in a standardized test can be a simple waste of educational resources, because they are not doing the intrinsically valuable learning that standardized tests are supposed to reveal. Teaching to a test designed to trigger learning and critical thinking as the best of the GCSEs are might be less problematic. And too much time spent teaching even to good tests has opportunity costs for valuable aspects of education that are not tested; in both countries the testing regimes may be crowding out physical education and some arts and music education which may be extremely valuable for preparing children for enjoying rewarding lives. But these criticisms are not specifically about the effects on the distribution of achievement or of educational resources. The concern about 'bubble kids' that concerns me is that teachers and schools concentrate resources on the children who are close to the threshold, at the expense of other children.

The expense falls on children at the further ends of the spectrum of measured achievement. In other words, children who are certain to do very well, or certain to do very badly, on the test in question get less attention than the children at or near the threshold ('proficiency' in the American case, the fifth C grade in GCSE in the United Kingdom). The diversion of resources away from children who are likely to do very well and towards students who are more marginal is to be welcomed from the egalitarian point of view, and although it would be objectionable if it ultimately undermined the long-term prospects of the least advantaged, given the actual governance structure of schooling, such a radical diversion of resources as would undermine the productiveness of the higher-achieving children is not a serious worry. By contrast, in so far as the focus on 'bubble kids' diverts resources from the lowest achievers, it has an inegalitarian dynamic. But many if not most interventions that target the less advantaged for the sake of equality redistribute resources among the less advantaged, and it is not always clear that they should be rejected on those grounds. This is a general problem for egalitarian reformers. Consider, for example, affirmative action. In our circumstances, at least in the short-to-medium term, there is a possibility that affirmative action, if effective, while benefiting some African Americans partly at the expense of some whites, also harms other African Americans by resulting in diminished social capital in their communities. If so, that is a count against affirmative action, but it does not amount to an all-things-considered case against affirmative action, because the benefits to the beneficiaries who are, ex hypothesi, harmed by the injustice which affirmative action is designed to repair, may outweigh the costs to others.

So the effects on the triaged children constitute a real moral cost, but not one that suffices in itself to justify condemning the system that leads to focus on the 'bubble kids'. Whether or not we should condemn the system from an egalitarian point of view depends on how valuable the benefits are to the 'bubble kids', and how serious the costs are to the triaged children. This, in turn, depends on the quality of what is learned. For example, if there is no real learning involved in being coached to proficiency, while the resources devoted to that coaching would otherwise have been devoted to bringing about genuine if small improvements to skills of the triaged students, then we should condemn it. If, on the other hand, the resources would have brought little benefit to the triaged children, and produce real gains in the skill levels of the 'bubble kids', then the case against is much weaker. Ultimately, of course, the egalitarian focus should be on redesigning accountability systems that create incentives for schools and teachers to focus resources across the spectrum of less-advantaged students.

## Concluding comments

Many more measures would probably help to raise low-end achievement. Experiments in extending the school day and the school year; designing extended school programmes so that they are not just drilling in basic skills, but resemble the kinds of experience that middle-class children have in the course of their out-of-school lives; devising schools-within-schools for low-achieving children who are identified as having potential; tutoring and volunteer programmes that deploy the resources of the local community; programmes educating parents on how more effectively to parent – these are all likely to play a part in comprehensive egalitarian reform. The Federal Department of Education in the USA has established a research program which allows for random-assignment experiments through which we shall surely learn a great deal about what works well in particular environments, and I hope that its UK counterpart will do more in this area. But I have refrained from offering a comprehensive egalitarian reform template. Attempting to do so in so short a piece would be impossible and presumptuous. Instead, I have offered comments on some of the key features of the education system from the perspective of concern about educational equality. I have restricted my attention to features of the existing system that I believe can be reformed without radical transformation either of the education system or of society more generally. I believe, in common with more radical critics, that to achieve a fully just society or system of schooling would require substantially more radical reform, but I do not see great prospects for such reform in the coming few decades; in the face of that prognosis I see no reason to refrain from advocating the smaller, and feasible, changes that would mitigate the educational inequality endemic in our social fabric.

## Notes

1. The intellectual influences on my thinking have been too numerous to mention. But I would like to acknowledge three people, and one institution, in particular. Adam Swift is my collaborator on most of my interesting philosophical work, and though he bears no responsibility for any of the errors in this piece, I owe him a great deal for getting the philosophical details as right as they are. Daily conversations with Lynn Glueck about the life of the schools she works in not only prompted me to enter the field of philosophy of education, but also have given me a much richer sense of the moral and practical issues surrounding educational justice than I could otherwise have had. Discussions over many years with Tim Brighouse have given me a great deal of respect for the value of implicit knowledge and its value in policymaking. Finally, I'm grateful to the Spencer Foundation for the diverse ways in which it has supported me in recent years.

2. The lower figure for urban districts is typically deceptively high. Urban districts typically educate higher proportions of students with disabilities, and among those with disabilities they have higher proportions of those with serious disabilities, than suburban schools; provision for such children is frequently well over $50,000 per year for districts in states which participate in IDEA which provides funds to states in return for those states imposing on districts stringent legal responsibilities to provide for students with disabilities. They are also typically responsible for larger proportions of students who must be educated in secure units. The Superintendent of a large urban district told me that her most expensive student costs her district $350,000 per year; he is educated by court order in a secure unit in another state, and her district is liable for the entire cost. The real spending on non-disabled non-criminal students within urban districts is typically, therefore, considerably lower than the nominal per-pupil figure.

3. For a more comprehensive discussion of the effects on equality of choice schemes in general see Geoff Whitty et al., *Devolution and Choice in Education* (1998), especially pp. 115–25.

4. I understand that 'eliminating the achievement gap' is not usually meant literally. The provisions of NCLB require only that no children achieve below a certain

threshold, and allow for inequality of achievement above that threshold – hence my invocation of the more explicit demands of British Education Secretaries.

5. This is a central theme of, for example, former Secretary of State Charles Clarke's speech to the Specialist Schools Trust, *Pupil-Centered Learning: Using Data to Improve Performance* (2003) and also of former Schools Minister David Miliband's IPPR pamphlet *Opportunity for All: Are We Nearly There Yet?* (2004).

6. See David Berliner, 'Our Impoverished View of Educational Reform'(2005) and Richard Rothstein, *Class and Schools* (2003) for nice accounts of ways in which non-educational reforms might be crucial to improving schools and why addressing child poverty might be especially important. For a rich account of the unequal preparedness of children to deal with school see Valerie E. Lee and David Burkham, *Inequality at the Starting Gate: Social Background Differences in Achievement as Children Begin School* (2003).

7. See Larry Temkin, 'The Levelling Down Objection to Equality'; T. M. Scanlon, 'The Diversity of Objections to Equality', and Harry Brighouse and Adam Swift, 'Equality, Priority, and Positional Goods', in *Ethics* (2006) and the first half of G. A. Cohen, *Rescuing Justice and Equality* (2008) for some arguments that equality per se does matter.

8. For the distinction between freedom and the freedoms we have a right to see Ronald Dworkin, *A Matter of Principle* (1985) chapter 9, and John Rawls's extensive discussion in 'The Basic Liberties and Their Priority' (1982).

9. See Cooper (1980) for an articulate presentation of this objection.

10. In 2000 the USA had a post-transfer child poverty rate of 21.9 per cent and the UK had a rate of 15.4 per cent compared with a post-transfer rate of 2.4 per cent, 2.8 per cent, 3.4 per cent and 4.2 per cent in Denmark, Finland, Norway and Sweden respectively.

11. See, for example, 'Lottery of school places backed' (BBC News Online, 2009) and 'School admissions lotteries should be promoted, councils told' (*The Daily Telegraph*, 2008). According to the latter story, nine Local Education Authorities were using lotteries in some form by late 2008.

12. For a rich and still-relevant study of the choice dynamic within large comprehensive high schools see the brilliant study by Arthur Powell, Eleanor Farrar and David Cohen, *The Shopping Mall High School: Winners and Losers in the Educational Marketplace* (1985).

13. Harvey Goldstein, personal communication, 2001. See also Harvey Goldstein, 'Value-Added Tables: The Less-than-holy Grail' (1997) pp. 18–19 and Harvey

Goldstein et al., *The Use of Value-Added Information in Judging School Performance* (2000).

14. For critical discussion of the understanding of proficiency see Richard Rothstein, *Class and Schools* (2004).

15. See also Booher-Jennings, Jennifer, 'Below the Bubble: "Educational Triage" and the Texas Accountability System' (2005).

## References

Ainsworth, J. (2002) 'Why Does It Take a Village? The Mediation of Neighborhood Effects on Educational Achievement', *Social Forces* 81, 1: 117–52.

BBC News Online (2009) 'Lottery of School Places Backed', at http://news.bbc.co.uk/2/hi/uk_news/education/4293446.stm (accessed on 20 January 2009, 9.47 a.m. Central Time)

Berliner, D. (2005) 'Our Impoverished View of Educational Reform', *Teachers College Record*, 108, 6: 949–95.

Betts, J. (2005) 'The Economic Theory of School Choice', in J. Betts (ed.) *Getting Choice Right* (Washington, DC: Brookings Institution).

Betts, J. and Roemer, J. (1998) 'Equalizing Educational Opportunity through Educational Finance Reform', at http://papers.ssrn.com/sol3/papers.cfm?abstract_id=214135 (accessed on 26 November 2009).

Biddle, B. and Berliner, D. (2003) 'What Research Says about Unequal Funding for Schools in America', *West Ed Policy Perspectives*, at http://www.wested.org/online_pubs/pp-03-01.pdf (accessed on 26 November 2009).

Booher-Jennings, J. (2005) 'Below the Bubble: "Educational Triage" and the Texas Accountability System', *American Education Research Journal*, 42: 231–68.

Brighouse, H. (2004) *Justice* (Cambridge: Polity Press).

Brighouse, H. and Swift, A. (2006a) 'Equality, Priority, and Positional Goods', *Ethics* 116, 3: 471–97.

—(2006b), 'Parents' Rights and the Value of the Family', *Ethics 117*, 1: 80–108.

—(2009) 'Legitimate Parental Partiality', *Philosophy and Public Affairs* 37, 1: 43–80.

Clarke, C. (2003) *Pupil-Centered Learning: Using Data to Improve Performance* (London: DFES).

Cohen, G. A. (2008) *Rescuing Justice and Equality* (Cambridge, MA: Harvard University Press).

Cooper, D. (1980) *Illusions of Equality* (London: Routledge and Kegan Paul).

*Daily Telegraph, The* (2008) 'School Admissions Lotteries Should Be Promoted, Councils Told', 9 October 2008, at http://www.telegraph.co.uk/education/3157997/School-admissions-lotteries-should-be-promoted-councils-told.html (accessed on 20 January 2009, 9.52 a.m. Central Time).

Davies, N. (1999a) 'Political Coup Bred Educational Disaster', *The Guardian*, 16 September.

—(1999b) 'Bias That Killed the Dream of Equality', *The Guardian,* 15 September.

Dworkin, R. (1985) *A Matter of Principle* (Cambridge, MA: Harvard University Press).

Freedman, S. and Horner, S. (2008) *School Funding and Social Justice* (London: Policy Exchange).

Gewirtz, S., Ball, S. J. and Bowe, R. (1995) *Markets, Choice and Equity in Education* (Buckingham: Open University Press).

Glazer, N. (2005) 'Separate and Unequal', *New York Times Book Review*, 25 September 2005.

Goldstein, H. (1997) 'Value-Added Tables: The Less-than-holy Grail', *Managing Schools Today* 6, 1.

Goldstein, H., Huiqi, P., Rath, T. and Hill, N. (2000) *The Use of Value-Added Information in Judging School Performance* (London: Institute of Education).

Lareau, A. (2003) *Unequal Childhoods* (Berkeley, CA: University of California Press).

Lee, S. (2005) *Up Against Whiteness* (New York: Teachers College Press).

Lee, Valerie E. and Burkham, D. (2003) *Inequality at the Starting Gate: Social Background Differences in Achievement as Children Begin School* (Washington, DC: Economic Policy Institute).

Lomasky, L. (1987) *Persons, Rights, and the Moral Community* (New York: Oxford University Press).

Miliband, David (2004) *Opportunity for All: Are We Nearly There Yet?* (London: IPPR).

Powell, A., Farrar, E. and Cohen, D. (1985) *The Shopping Mall High School: Winners and Losers in the Educational Marketplace* (Wilmington, MA: Houghton Mifflin).

Rawls, J. (1982) 'The Basic Liberties and Their Priority', in Sterling M. McMurrin (ed.) *The Tanner Lectures on Human Values, III* (Salt Lake City, UT: University of Utah Press), pp. 1–87.

—(2001) *Justice as Fairness* (Cambridge, MA: Harvard University Press).

Rothstein, R. (2004) *Class and Schools* (Washington, DC: Economic Policy Institute).

—(2008) 'Whose Problem Is Poverty?', *Educational Leadership* 65, 7: 8–13.

Rothstein, R., Jacobson, R. and Wilder, T. (2008) *Grading Education: Getting Accountability Right* (New York: EPI/Teachers College Press).

Scanlon, T. M. (2003) 'The Diversity of Objections to Inequality', in T. M. Scanlon, *The Difficulty of Tolerance: Essays in Political Philosophy* (Cambridge: Cambridge University Press).

Temkin, L. (2000) 'Equality Priority and the Levelling-Down Objection', in M. Clayton and A. Williams (eds) *The Ideal of Equality* (Basingstoke: Macmillan).

Thomas Fordham Institute (2006) *Fund the Child: Tackling Inequity and Antiquity in School Finance*, at http://www.edexcellence.net/fundthechild/Manifesto%20 Report.pdf (accessed 14 December 2009 at 20.06 Central Time).

US Census Bureau, Public Education Finances (2006) at http://ftp2.census.gov/govs/ school/06f33pub.pdf (accessed on 26 November 2009).

de Vise, D. (2007) 'A Concentrated Approach to Exams: Rockville School's Efforts Raise Questions of Test-prep Ethics', *Washington Post*, 4 March 2007, at http://www. washingtonpost.com/wp-dyn/content/article/2007/03/03/AR2007030301372. html?nav=rss_education (accessed on 27 April 2009 at 13.00 Central Time).

Whitty, G., Power, S. and Halpin, D. (1998) *Devolution and Choice in Education: The School, the State and the Market* (Buckingham: Open University Press).

Wilson, J. (1991) 'Does Equality (of Opportunity) Make Sense in Education?' *Journal of Philosophy of Education* 25, 1: 27–32.

www.boldapproach.org (accessed on 22 November 2009).

www.dfes.gov.uk/performancetables (accessed on 22 November 2009).

# Educational Equality in the Shadow of the Reagan Era    **2**

Kenneth R. Howe

> ## Chapter Outline
>

## Introduction

I accepted the invitation to comment on Harry Brighouse's 'Educational Equality and School Reform' without a second thought. Harry is a leading thinker on matters of educational equality, and I am honoured to join him in this volume. With the exception of school choice policy, I didn't anticipate there would be many differences in our views. But I was mistaken. I often find the prospects for greater educational equality to be more remote and more fraught with obstacles than Harry seems to. Because Harry and I share a similarly strong commitment to equality, there is a lesson here about the looseness of fit between a general philosophical orientation and real world education policy.

The organization of my commentary parallels the organization of Harry's essay, with one exception. I do not have a separate subsection on admissions policies because I think the issues raised are addressed in my coverage of choice. I restrict myself almost exclusively to the US education policy scene, a restriction that should be understood unless I indicate otherwise.

## How education systems contribute to inequality

Brighouse devotes his opening section on how the US and UK education systems contribute to inequality primarily to funding and choice, both of which he revisits in subsequent sections. I have no disagreements with what he says about funding in the USA, although I think it might have been useful for him to have provided some mention of the issue of *adequacy* versus *equalization* standards for funding that has received some play in the USA and that is particularly relevant to the question of whether educational outcomes should be equalized as opposed to (formal) educational opportunities. The adequacy standard differentiates funding based on what is required to bring children of different needs up to some substantive performance standard. It is more egalitarian than simply equalizing funding for students, though its practicability and legal status are currently quite uncertain.

I do disagree with several things Brighouse says about choice, at least as they apply to the USA. For example, he rightly points out that neighbourhood schooling is itself a variety of school choice, namely, choosing a school by choosing a place of residence. In this way parents can collude to exclude less-advantaged students from their preferred schools. But he wrongly asserts that parents who send their children to charter schools cannot also collude to keep out the disadvantaged. Charter schools and parents can and do collude in all sorts of ways, from actively recruiting high-performing students (sometimes creating a large pool from which they then *randomly select*), to requiring parents to provide 'sweat equity' in the form of work at their child's school, to adopting admissions preferences for children with legacies, to steering away special-education students for 'lack of fit', to not having free and reduced price lunch programmes, to having explicitly selective admissions for gifted charter schools.[1] Indeed, laying a choice system over a neighbourhood school system can provide an additional and easier way for parents to engage in 'white flight' from neighbourhood schools.

Brighouse cites studies by Davies and Gewirtz et al. that identify similar tendencies towards inequality resulting from the 1988 Education Reform Act in the United Kingdom. But he urges caution about these findings for three reasons. First, the same people are advantaged by the new system as the old and the question whether they are more so is an open question. Second, a good deal of time has passed since the data was collected. Third, the Labour government has since introduced major reforms. The second and third reasons do not apply to the USA. Research is ongoing and the results pretty firmly establish that, in general, excluding magnet schools with a mission of integration, public school choice is having no appreciable effect on overall achieve-ment (charter schools are exacerbating inequality for low-income children) (see National Assessment of Educational Progress 2005; Lubienski and Lubienski, 2006; Robelson, 2008); and either has no effect on segregation by class and race or, depending on the district and State, exacerbates it. Regarding the answer to the question of whether the previously advantaged are more advantaged with the advent of formal school choice systems, I would say it is quite likely 'yes'. With the exception of targeted voucher systems, the expansion of school choice in the USA has exacted no costs on advantaged parents while further enabling those so disposed to segregate their children from more needy children (Howe and Eisenhart, 2000; Frankenberg and Lee, 2003; Orfield and Lee, 2006).

## What is educational equality and why does it matter?

The principle of educational equality matters, according to Brighouse, because it promotes fairness, in particular, fair competition for goods to which education serves as the gateway, such as income, wealth, status and the self-fulfilment that flows from these. This is not a controversial claim in the USA. A general commitment to the principle of educational equality, however, leaves quite open the questions of how to conceive it more precisely, as well as how to weigh it against competing principles with which it may conflict.

Brighouse proffers two general conceptions of the principle of educational equality: 'meritocratic' and 'radical'. These conceptions differ in terms of what they construe to be morally permissible sources of educational inequality. The meritocratic conception permits educational inequality to result from differences in talent and effort but not from social class background. The radical conception permits less. It adds talent (and apparently that portion of effort that is owed to social class background) to social class background as a morally impermissible source of educational inequality. Both conceptions permit educational inequality to track differences in effort with the possible exception noted above.

Brighouse observes that the meritocratic conception is very demanding, in two ways: (1) it requires considerably more resources to educate children from lower social class backgrounds; and (2) it requires substantially reducing socio-economic inequalities that result in educational inequalities that outstrip the abilities of schools to overcome on their own. Even so, Brighouse suggests, the meritocratic conception may not be demanding enough. The radical conception may be required because the level of effort children put forth in school is associated with their social class backgrounds and because no one can claim credit for their natural endowments, these factors, too, should be placed with social class background among the impermissible sources of educational inequality.

Both of Brighouse's conceptions are problematic, in my view. His meritocratic conception is considerably more demanding – more egalitarian – than the conception of merit that has its home in the rhetorical context of educational policy-making. Given my reading of that context, social class per se is deemed a morally impermissible source of educational inequality, but what typically flows from it by way of academic *talent* is not. For many critics in education, setting policy on the basis of the principle of merit embraces the 'myth' of meritocracy, a myth used to rationalize inequality. The principle of merit is identified with formal equality of opportunity, or non-discrimination, whereby the talented among the poor are identified and provided with the opportunity to develop those *talents*, thereby increasing the overall *talent* pool – a general idea nowadays often conceived in terms of the principle of maximizing human capital. My point here is not to suggest that Brighouse has gotten the meritocratic conception wrong, philosophically speaking, much less to defend human capital theory as a guide to educational policy. Rather, it is to suggest that Brighouse's conception is philosophically freighted and is likely to be mistaken for the more formalist conception of meritocracy described above that is often used in the broader education policy conversation. He might do better to label his meritocratic conception the *substantive meritocratic conception* or perhaps the *fair educational equality conception*.

There is a similar rhetorical problem regarding Brighouse's use of the concept of talent, which explains my use of italics in the preceding paragraph. It is not altogether clear whether Brighouse's conception of talent encompasses *acquired talent* in addition to *natural talent*, but it appears not. Otherwise, he wouldn't be able to distinguish talent from social class background and add it to the morally impermissible sources of educational inequality in his radical conception of educational quality. But in most cases it is very difficult to distinguish between acquired and natural talent on the basis of observed performance. One important reason is that natural talents must be developed, and often in a timely manner, lest the prospects for realizing their manifestation fade. Another is the age-old problem of isolating and determining the mix of nature and nurture that goes into human performance, which has played out most notoriously in IQ testing. If one insists that the idea of acquired talent is just wrong-headed, then the same sort of practical difficulties of identification arise with respect to distinguishing *latent* from *manifest* talent.

As in the case of his conception of merit, Brighouse's conception of talent is likely different from how it is generally understood in the education policy arena, where, I surmise, it is construed more in terms of its stability (resistance to change) and how well it predicts subsequent performance than in terms of its genesis. And that conception fits very comfortably with the human capital framework described above, which is considerably less demanding of educational equality than Brighouse's framework.

Despite these difficulties, the general idea of natural talent can be a plausible and useful one. This is particularly so in the case of disability, where it is possible to identify 'natural' factors that go into an individuals' performance that are beyond their power to control and with respect to which they cannot be held responsible, Down's syndrome, for example. But it is a bit puzzling why Brighouse would associate this observation about natural talents with a 'radical' conception of educational equality in connection with US special-education policy. The idea of natural talents serves as much – more – to set limits on what is required in the name of educational equality as it does to provide an impetus to overcome inequality.[2] In the case of school children with disabilities, although the institution of special education requires responding to special needs, it also often adopts more limited academic goals that are set out in 'individualized educational programs' (IEPs) tailored to natural talents.

Including the requirement to overcome the limitations and advantages that flow from natural talents in a conception of educational equality is radical indeed, so much so that it is beyond the pale.[3] That perhaps explains why Brighouse pretty much drops it in favour of the meritocratic conception, which, in the current context for US education policy-making is plenty radical enough. That context is characterized by marked scepticism regarding the political legitimacy of government programmes as well as their capacity to improve the prospects of the disadvantaged, coupled with a denial that occupying a low position in the socio-economic structure should serve as an explanation of – an *excuse for* – poor school performance. Growing quite naturally out of these premises is an approach to educational policy that isolates the institution of schooling from the social and economic structures surrounding it. The actors within the institution of schooling – educators, children and parents – are the source of responsibility, praise and blame for academic performance, and the proper target of policy instruments. This is not a context in which the (substantive) meritocratic conception can get much traction.

## How *much* does educational equality matter?

In a pluralistic, liberal-democratic society, the principle of educational equality is bound to come into conflict with other values and thus must be weighed against them. Brighouse considers three such values: family values, educational excellence and benefiting the least advantaged.

1. *Family values* Brighouse argues that it is a mistake to deny, as some egalitarians do, that freedom is at stake when parents'

educational choices on behalf of their children are restricted in the interests of educational equality. In his view, the principle of educational equality does restrict parents' freedom but there is nothing unconditionally objectionable about this because all freedoms are restricted in some way. Educational equality is associated with fairness and in many cases 'fairness trumps freedom'. Among the policies Brighouse defends on these grounds are prohibiting elite private schools, desegregating by race or class and abolishing academic selection.

The 'burden of proof', according to Brighouse, 'is on the opponent of the measure supporting equality' (p. 35) to show that it violates a '*basic* liberty' required by justice. He believes this burden is met in the case of the strong interest shared by children and parents alike in maintaining the intimate relationships that are made possible by no institution other than family. Given the nature of the interests at stake here, the pursuit of educational equality may be curtailed. For example, the pursuit of equality should not go to the extreme of limiting how much time parents may spend with their children reading to them, in order to prevent those children from gaining an educational advantage. And the same principle of non-interference applies to parents imparting values, enthusiasms and religious beliefs, provided these are not harmful to children nor imparted by indoctrination.

This principle of non-interference in the parent–child relationship can be pretty difficult to apply in individual cases, for example, the Amish. But all principles encounter hard cases. The more general difficulty in my view is that thinkers on the right, and maybe even many in what counts for the middle these days, would likely disagree with Brighouse's claim that the 'burden of proof' is on those who oppose equality when it conflicts with parental freedom. It would be useful to have some more precise way to make the determination of when Brighouse's burden is met. For example, what's to prevent expanding the non-interference principle to permit elite private schools on the grounds that maintaining intimacy with *adult* children requires that children whose parents had an elite education, and were shaped by all that involves, also need an elite education in order to be similarly shaped? (I may be demanding too much here. Perhaps Brighouse provides a more precise argument in the collaborative work with Swift to which he refers in his essay.)

2. *Educational excellence* Brighouse makes a quite useful distinction between individual educational excellence and the excellence of an educational system. Individual excellence brings to mind 'perfectionism'. Certain intellectual skills have intrinsic value, and those who possess the capability and interest needed to develop such skills should be supported in doing so by the education system. Brighouse affirms the existence of intrinsic educational values, but he also believes that in a just education system they are overridden by the value of educational equality. He is right about both in my view. But promoting the excellence of an education system has been and continues to be a much more central issue in the education policy arena than promoting individual excellence. Indeed, at least since the National Commission on Educational Excellence produced *A Nation at Risk*, in 1983, excellence of the educational system has been front and centre.

*A Nation at Risk* – a product of political climate of the time – helped drive a wedge between educational excellence and educational equality. Then President Ronald Reagan suggested that too much had been done in the name of equality, and too fast. His administration made a significant retreat from the pursuit of equality, including significantly cutting funding (Salamone, 1986). The alignment of educational excellence with economic goals also helped spur the ascendance of a rough-and-ready form of utilitarian human capital theory (UHCT) as a guide to education policy making (Strike, 1985). UHCT poses a significant challenge to Brighouse's intuitions about the trade-offs between equality and the total good produced in excellent educational systems.

UHCT construes education to be an investment from which returns, namely, economically valuable knowledge and skills, should be maximized. One can't tell which of Brighouse's hypothetical education systems (p. 40) would be judged most excellent by UHCT because we need a least two additional kinds of information: (1) what the numbers in the example signify in terms of the level of economically valuable knowledge and skills and (2) what proportion of people a system develops in each category of economically valuable skills. Consider the following two systems:

| | System A | | System B | |
|---|---|---|---|---|
| Employment Category | Student % | Econ. utility | Student % | Econ. utility |
| Prof/Tech (5 utility pts) | 35 | 175 | 10 | 50 |
| Skilled (3 utility pts) | 35 | 105 | 72 | 216 |
| Semi-skilled (1 utility pt) | 15 | 15 | 18 | 18 |
| Unskilled (0 utility pts) | 15 | 0 | 0 | 0 |
| Total econ. utility: | | 295 | | 284 |

In this example, System A has considerably more inequality than System B but is superior in terms of maximizing economically valuable skills and thus more excellent in terms of a UHCT framework. It could increase or decrease its margin over System B, depending on how relatively productive the mix of the percentages in the employment categories. But this issue is rarely, if ever, addressed in a systematic way in education policy-making. The strategy, instead, is to push for uniformly high standards – *college for all* policies, and the like – with the ostensive goal of raising all boats. It pays little attention to how raising standards without also providing adequate opportunities to learn leaves disadvantaged students by the wayside. (I'll return to this issue in the section on accountability.)

The problem with Brighouse's view is not what he says about educational excellence, but what he doesn't say. Among the challenges to equality in the name of promoting educational excellence, the UHCT policy framework poses the strongest. It has become a driving force in US education policy-making up to and including the No Child Left Behind Act (NCLB). It sanctions an unacceptable level of educational inequality and, ultimately, social and economic inequality as well.

3. *Benefiting the least advantaged* As with family values, Brighouse ranks benefiting the least advantaged – including those with severe disabilities, low income, or low status – ahead of educational equality. One might think that the least advantaged could not benefit from an arrangement that directed resources away from them and towards the more advantaged. But the least advantaged might benefit more in the long run by having educational resources distributed towards the more academically talented than by receiving the resources themselves. For example, distributing more educational resources towards the more academically talented might result in the development of new gene therapies to help treat or eliminate various disabilities, and so forth. And distributing educational resources in this way might be accomplished by permitting elite private schools. To the extent that such an arrangement would develop human capital that would benefit the long run prospects of the least advantaged, Brighouse believes it is warranted, despite the fact it would violate the meritocratic conception of educational equality by disadvantaging those unable to attend the elite private schools who possess levels of talent and motivation similar to those who are able to attend.

One can agree with Brighouse's strong commitment to benefiting the least advantaged but disagree with his views on how to respond to it. Assuming that elite private schools would benefit the least advantaged in the way hypothesized, benefiting the least advantaged does not have to be put into direct conflict with educational equality if educational equality is given a different interpretation. In particular, Amy Gutmann's *threshold* conception of educational equality does not require that there be no relationship between social class background and educational performance, as Brighouse's meritocratic conception does, but it requires that the influence of social class background be sufficiently limited so that all children (with exceptions such as the cognitively or emotionally impaired) receive an education up to a threshold that enables 'effective participation' in the political system (Gutmann, 1999). Beyond the threshold, various individuals and communities may pursue further education at their discretion. There are problems in specifying the threshold, of course, and Gutmann arguably gives far too little attention to economic considerations. But the general framework is a very useful and powerful one that reinterprets the principle of educational equality in a less demanding way than Brighouse but then does not have to trade it off to benefit the least advantaged.

Gutmann's framework permits private schools to exist along side public schools on the grounds they permit (or should permit) parental discretion only so far as it does not have the consequence of pushing other children under the threshold. And as a practical matter, private schools have historically functioned as a safety valve for the release of pressure built up from dissatisfied parents. It is unwise policy to severely restrict citizens' freedom to pursue their perceived interests when not outweighed by identifiable harm, a principle that also leads countries with socialized medicine to permit private health care.[4] But should students attending private schools gain such a large advantage that they threaten to put those who reach the pre-existing threshold at a significant disadvantage, the threshold for public education must be adjusted. Presumably, Brighouse would hold a similar view regarding elite private schools. That is, at some point, it seems, the gap between the quality of education provided to children in public schools and that provided to similarly talented and motivated children in elite private schools would be unacceptably large. (It is likely already so for many public schools.)

With respect to the least advantaged, where feasible, additional resources should be allocated to bring them up to the threshold. Where not feasible, they should receive an education tailored to enabling them to make the most of their abilities and, consistent with the general thrust of Rawls' difference principle, should subsequently be provided with social supports they need to, in Brighouse's words, 'maximize the prospects for flourishing' (p. 43). This approach has the advantage over the hoped-for spin-off benefits of human capital development of focusing directly on how to think about educational equality and its limits in the case of the least advantaged.

Finally, the value of educational equality is rendered generally precarious by Brighouse's view that permits it to be overridden by the value of educational excellence (in the form of the developing of human capital), even if constrained by the value of benefiting the least advantaged. I doubt that Brighouse would want this result and thus am not sure I've properly understood him. But I see nothing to prevent the same reasoning that Brighouse employs to justify permitting elite private schools from also being employed to justify practices within the public schools that further advantage the already advantaged – such as talent tracking and selective admissions on the part of public schools of choice – on the grounds that such practices develop more human capital, more efficiently. Once the efficient development of human capital is permitted to justify the suspension of the requirement for educational equality, I see no principled barrier to using it to justify policies benefiting talented and motivated, easy to educate students on that ground. Moreover, the requirement to benefit the least advantaged is a very weak constraint in the first place, for the connection between the development of human capital by elite private schools and betterment of the prospects of the least advantaged is quite speculative. Indeed, although the fruits of human capital – from antibiotics to safer automobiles – have benefited the least advantaged to some degree, they have most benefited the most advantaged. But even in a relatively more just society, the benefits of developing human capital would seem to be quite diffuse and not specifically linked to any given stratum of society. Measures directly targeted at the least advantaged would seem to be a much more promising approach to benefiting them than a scattershot human capital approach.[5]

## Moving towards educational equality

Following his general discussion of trade-offs between educational equality and competing values of family, Brighouse sets the stage for his examination of specific educational policy reforms. Drawing on the work of Arnette Lareau and Richard Rothstein,[6] he emphasizes the limited capacity of school reform alone to bring about educational equality. He concludes that it is 'naïve' to hope educational equality can be achieved through measures that focus only on schools. On the other hand, although what can be achieved by school reform alone is limited, the prospects for a more comprehensive approach are not on the political horizon. Thus, it is not 'quixotic' to pursue school-oriented reforms.

Quixotic or not, school-oriented reform is all that is in the offing for the foreseeable future. So I agree with Brighouse that we ought to pursue that avenue. On the other hand, we should do so in a way that doggedly keeps the issue of limits on the table. Unlike Brighouse, I am not surprised that people so often express scepticism about whether extra-school factors affect educational equality. But I suspect the scepticism is not just about the factual matter of whether extra-school factors are related to school performance – otherwise, it's hard to see why the elite devote so much effort to manipulating these factors – but also about the moral matter of what, if anything, ought to be done to mitigate them. Those who deny the need for a more comprehensive approach often have more to answer for than naïveté. As Rothstein says (in the same piece Brighouse cites), 'There's a lack of moral, political, and intellectual integrity in [the] suppression of awareness of how social and economic disadvantage lowers achievement' (Rothstein, 2008, p. 9).

## Funding

Brighouse focuses his discussion of school funding on the idea of differentiating or weighting funding according to student need. The most needy children receive the highest level of funding and the least needy children, the lowest level. I agree with Brighouse that weighted student funding (WSF) promotes the value of educational equality, at least potentially. But I believe its capacity to do so is quite dependent on other education policies that are in place along with it, particularly choice and accountability systems.

Brighouse cites the Netherlands as having a long-standing system of WSF in conjunction with its choice policy. But what we need to know about that system is whether it has fostered greater educational equality. There are grounds for significant doubt. According to work by Karsten et al., the choice system is a significant factor in the social class and ethnic segregation that characterizes Dutch schools (Karsten et al., 2006), and Brighouse agrees that educational equality is a powerful enough value to outweigh parental freedom if it promotes segregation. New Zealand also had weighted student funding as part of its relatively unrestricted school choice system in the late 1990s and also experienced significant social class and ethnic segregation attributable to the system (see Lauder and Hughs, 1999; Fisk and Ladd, 2000).

In the USA, fundraising can easily undermine the egalitarian goal of WSF/choice systems. Parents can choose to send their low-funded/high-performing children to schools with similar students and then simply add to the government provided resources available to their children through fundraising specifically for their schools.

It is difficult to know how fundraising would affect the outcome of the auction scheme Brighouse asks us to consider. Perhaps parents of high performing children would be willing to accept a very large gap between per-pupil funding for their children and disadvantaged children and make up the difference with fundraising. I doubt it, for I believe they would be more likely to demand equal funding, as many have in the school district in which I reside that has provided extra funding to schools with high proportions of disadvantaged students. In any case, the auction scheme would surely be affected by the accountability system that was in place. If accountability was relatively weak such that it set no minimum standard of proficiency that schools would have to achieve for disadvantaged children, then the schools' response might be to enrol a relatively large proportion of disadvantaged children and use a portion of the additional funding to subsidize the educational experience of high performing children. If schools were held strictly accountable for producing a relatively high standard of proficiency for disadvantaged students, they would likely avoid them given any level of additional funding that is currently feasible. Under the current NCLB system, for example, they would eventually be forced to reconstitute their schools for failing to produce the required level of achievement.

Related to the second horn of this dilemma, WSF shares a real world problem with the *adequacy* criterion of educational funding. In contrast to the *equalization* criterion, the adequacy criterion establishes differential levels of funding required for differently advantaged students to meet some substantive achievement level. The problem that the adequacy criterion and WSF share is encouraging the idea that educational equality might be achieved if sufficient resources are poured into the schools.[7] But this ignores the profound influence of extra-school resources and sets schools up for failure, and when they do fail, encourages setting a limit on the degree of educational equality that is attainable short of where it should be set. And it also feeds into the *funding doesn't matter* rhetoric that encourages relatively cheap, quick-fix educational reforms such as choice and punitive accountability systems.

## Choice

Brighouse sees a 'very strong, and regrettable, tendency on the left to see choice as the enemy of equality' (p. 54). I possess that tendency I take it, but not because I'm hidebound. My marked scepticism about the capacity of school choice to promote greater educational equality has much more to do with the contingencies of on-the-ground educational policy-making – including the genesis of school-choice policy and the outcomes it has produced – than with philosophical principle (Howe, 2008).

Brighouse cannot be accurately described as a school-choice enthusiast. His support for choice is conditional and his expectations for it limited. He requires only that it do better at producing educational equality than feasible alternatives. In this vein, he argues that school assignment by neighbourhood is massively unjust and, moreover, is itself a form of school choice. Formal school-choice systems, he contends, do not introduce choice, they redistribute choice. Brighouse admits that choice systems may redistribute choice in ways that further exacerbate educational inequality, such as inter-district choice in which transportation is not provided. But he also sees other systems that have potential to foster greater equality: targeted vouchers for low-income children, requiring all parents to participate in choice, providing free transportation and limiting the ability of schools to select students.

In point of fact, none of Brighouse's suggestions have taken hold in a significant way. Although targeted vouchers have garnered significant attention, they serve an exceedingly small number of children and have done little to foster greater equality in any case.[8] Requiring all parents to participate in choice and providing free transportation are very uncommon features of choice systems, and their effectiveness is likely to be quite limited.[9] Limiting the ability of schools to select students is a formal feature of charter schools, a large and growing form of school choice in the USA, but is frequently subverted.[10] Charter schools have failed to foster more equal achievement – worse, have sometimes widened the achievement gap – and charter schools also have a tendency to exacerbate various forms of segregation.[11]

School choice has little potential to foster greater educational equality given current political undercurrents. Brighouse's rationale and criterion for evaluating school choice is egalitarian. But since its beginnings as a genuine policy option in the Reagan administration, actual school-choice policy in the USA has been grounded in the value of parental autonomy, viewed both as an intrinsic good and as an instrumental good conducive to producing the maximum overall excellence of the system. In this context, 'freedom trumps fairness', and egalitarian reforms are routinely resisted or subverted. If school choice is to foster greater educational equality, tinkering around the edges won't work. A reordering of fundamental political values is required.[12]

## Accountability

Brighouse's description of the NCLB Act as introducing 'moderate accountability requirements' took me aback. I suspect many others would be taken aback as well. If you take the goal NCLB sets seriously – that all children at all levels of schooling shall be 'proficient' in math and literacy by 2014 (12 years from when the Act took effect) – and the penalties on schools for failing to make Adequate Yearly Progress towards this goal, including be forced to close or reconstitute themselves – NCLB seems anything but moderate. Indeed, at the time, I called it 'preposterous', and I haven't changed my mind. But perhaps Brighouse means NCLB is moderate in terms of the scope of the individuals and institutions it holds accountable.

Be that as it may, I am in pretty close agreement with what Brighouse says about some form of accountability being necessary, disaggregating student achievement by socio-economic and ethnic groups, and the correct egalitarian response to 'bubble kids'. As in the case of his discussion of educational excellence, the problems I have are with what he doesn't say. These problems could be among the badly designed features of NCLB that Brighouse thinks require dramatic fixing. Fine. In this vein, I should acknowledge that Brighouse does emphasize the general importance of incentives that encourage focusing resources on the disadvantaged, a point that figures prominently in my critical observations, especially the second.

One of the central egalitarian criticisms of educational accountability systems in the USA, of which NCLB is the latest and most far-reaching example, is that they ignore so-called 'opportunity to learn' standards.[13] That is, they put standards in place for which schools are held accountable but provide far too little additional resources to give schools a realistic chance of succeeding in terms of them. This raises serious questions about just how serious the commitment is to the avowed goal of closing the achievement gap. Related to the 'bubble kid' issue, standards/test-based accountability systems also place an especially heavy burden on teachers and principals in schools that serve disadvantaged students, and one of their primary responses has been to emphasize tested skills and propositional knowledge at the expense of higher order skills and more sophisticated forms of knowledge. Such systems have also been shown to increase dropout rates (McNeil, 2000; McNeil et al., 2008). The upshot is that accountability systems such as NCLB further disadvantage children who are already disadvantaged in the education system.

Brighouse is also silent on the punitive nature of accountability systems like NCLB that create incentive systems of questionable effectiveness – 'While you can beat people into submission, you can't beat them into greatness' (Houston, 2007) – and that encourage teachers and principals to leave or refuse to go to struggling schools because being at such schools puts their jobs in jeopardy. Finally, and following my own advice to be dogged about keeping the importance of extra-school factors on the table:

> Closing or substantially narrowing achievement gaps requires combining school improvement with reforms that narrow the vast

socioeconomic inequalities in the United States. Without such a combination, demands (like those of No Child Left Behind) that schools fully close achievement gaps not only will remain unfulfilled, but also will cause us to foolishly and unfairly condemn our schools and teachers. (Rothstein, 2008, pp. 8–9)

## Concluding comments

On the occasion of receiving *A Nation at Risk*, in April 1983, then President Reagan made the following remarks:

[O]ur educational system is in the grip of a crisis caused by low standards, lack of purpose, ineffective use of resources, and a failure to challenge students to push performance to the boundaries of individual ability – and that is to strive for excellence . . .

[The] call for an end to Federal intrusion is consistent with our task of redefining the Federal role in education. I believe that parents, not government, have the primary responsibility for the education of their children. Parental authority is not a right conveyed by the state; rather, parents delegate to their elected school board representatives and State legislators the responsibility for their children's schooling . . .

So, we'll continue to work in the months ahead for passage of tuition tax credits, vouchers, educational savings accounts, voluntary school prayer and abolishing the Department of Education. Our agenda is to restore quality to education by increasing competition and by strengthening parental choice and local control. . . . (Reagan, 1983)

This legacy continues to drive education policy-making in the USA. The refusal to recognize and acknowledge the fundamental importance of extra-school resources for school performance, which naturally combines with its unyielding commitment to market-driven/punitive accountability education reforms, casts a long and dark shadow over educational policy-making seriously committed to educational equality.

But the USA also has an earlier, fundamentally egalitarian, legacy. Its principles – which are quite congenial to Brighouse's meritocratic conception of educational equality – were articulated by the then President Lyndon Johnson, himself a former teacher of disadvantaged children:

> [A]bility is not just the product of birth. Ability is stretched or stunted by the family that you live with, and the neighborhood you live in – by the school you go to and the poverty or the richness of your surroundings. It is the product of a hundred unseen forces playing upon the little infant, the child, and finally the man . . .
>
> [I]t is not enough to open the gates of opportunity; all our citizens must have the ability to walk through those gates . . . We seek not just legal equity but human ability, not just equality as a right and a theory but equality as a fact and equality as a result . . .
>
> We are trying to attack [inequality] through our poverty program, through our education program, through our medical care and our other health programs, and a dozen more of the Great Society programs that are aimed at the root causes of this poverty.
>
> We will increase, and we will accelerate, and we will broaden this attack in years to come until this most enduring of foes finally yields to our unyielding will. (Johnson, 1965)

The education and surrounding welfare programmes enacted and spurred by Johnson's 'Great Society' had many flaws, to be sure, but to abandon educational equality as a central value, as happened in the Reagan Era, was to abandon the fundamental value that everyone should have a fair chance at life. Perhaps in the light of the new administration in the USA the necessary reordering of values can take place and our egalitarian legacy can re-emerge from the shadow that has been cast upon it for too long.

## Notes

1. All of these methods for excluding disadvantaged students except charter schools exclusively for the gifted (which I know to exist in several other Colorado school districts) were documented in a study of the Boulder Valley School District I spearheaded in 2000 (see Howe and Eisenhart, 2000). The district includes a number of non-charter choice schools, 'focus schools', that have no catchment area and in

other ways have the same formal admissions policies as charter schools. They also exhibit selectivity. No significant changes in Boulder choice policy have resulted from the 2000 study and segregation continues apace. Whatever the mechanisms, patterns of enrolment consistent with the exclusion of disadvantaged and relatively more disadvantaged children from charter schools occur across Colorado (see Howe, 2006). The patterns also occur across the nation (see Frankenberg and Lee, 2003; Carnoy et al., 2005; Orfield and Lee, 2006).

2. This is how I see natural talent operating in Rawls' theory. 'Fair equality of opportunity' by itself leaves room for an unacceptably high degree of inequality in primary goods that flow from differences in natural talents. This potential level of inequality is constrained by the 'difference principle'.

3. Brighouse subsequently concedes that, to be plausible, the radical conception must be weighed against other values (Brighouse, pp. 33–4), making it unacceptable, for example, to lobotomize more talented students to render less talented students equal. I think it would be a good idea for Brighouse to include a ceteris paribus or feasibility clause in his formulation of the radical conception.

4. The argument about whether to permit private schools is pretty much moot with respect to actual policy in the USA where private schools have a constitutional right to exist. See *Pierce v. Society of Sisters* (1925).

5. Such programmes are common. A particularly interesting example is affirmative action for members of groups likely to use the fruits of their education to serve disadvantaged communities. African American physicians, for example, are more likely than white physicians to do this. Thus, given the aim of serving disadvantaged communities, African Americans should be given preference in admission of medical and law schools. At first blush, this may seem to compromise educational equality, but not if serving disadvantaged communities is construed as a qualification for admission, along side other qualifications related to the welfare of the citizenry (see Dworkin, 1978).

6. In *Class and Schools* (2004), Rothstein reinforces the findings of celebrated Coleman Report of 1966, often interpreted to imply that schools don't make a difference. Rothstein labels this a mistake, and interprets the Coleman Report, correctly in my view, to imply that schools don't make enough of a difference, not even close to enough, to overcome the social advantages/disadvantages of children attributable to outside of school factors.

7. This criticism of the adequacy criterion is from Rothstein, 2004.

8. The longest standing and most intensively studied voucher program, the Milwaukee Parental Choice Program, continues to show no ability to produce

higher achievement than public schools (see Witte et al., 2009). For a general analysis of vouchers, see Belfield and Levin, 2005.

9. These measures are likely to be quite limited in their capacity to overcome the kinds of factors that affect school choice documented in the study by Gewirtz et al., cited by Brighouse.

10. See note 1.

11. See note 2.

12. Traditional magnet schools that have equality as central to their mission – that reorder excellence and equality – are one form of school choice that shows promise to promote equality. Unfortunately, federal government support is being diverted to charter schools that show no such promise (see Frankenberg and Siegel-Hawley, 2008.)

13. See Howe, 1994, for a discussion how 'opportunity to learn' standards lost out in 1994 in an earlier reauthorization of the 1965 Elementary and Secondary Education Act of which NCLB is the latest.

## References

Belfield, C. and Levin, H. M. (2005) 'Vouchers and Public Policy: When Ideology Trumps Evidence', *American Journal of Education*, 111: 548–67.

Carnoy, M., Jacobsen, R., Michel, L. and Rothstein, R. (2005) *The Charter School Dust-Up* (Washington, DC: Economic Policy Institute and Teachers College Press).

Dworkin, R. (1978) 'Reverse Discrimination', in R. Dworkin, *Taking Rights Seriously* (Cambridge, MA: Harvard University Press).

Fiske, E. and Ladd, H. (2000) *When Schools Compete: A Cautionary Tale* (Washington, DC: The Brookings Institution).

Frankenberg, E. and Lee, Chungmei (2003) *Charter Schools and Race: A Lost Opportunity for Integrated Education* (Cambridge, MA: The Civil Rights Project at Harvard University).

Frankenberg, E. and Siegel-Hawley, G. (2008) 'The Forgotten Choice? Rethinking Magnet Schools in a Changing Landscape', *The Civil Rights Project*, at http://www.civilrightsproject.ucla.edu/ (accessed on 22 November 2009).

Gutmann, A. (1999) *Democratic Education* (Princeton, NJ: Princeton University Press).

Houston, P. (2007) 'The Seven Deadly Sins of No Child Left Behind', *Phi Delta Kappan* 88, 10: 744–8, esp. 747.

Howe, K. (1994) 'Standards, Assessment, and Equality of Educational Opportunity', *Educational Researcher* 23, 8: 27–33.

—(2006) 'An Appraisal of Colorado's Charter Schools: Implications for Redirecting Policy', *Prism* 5, 1: 9–12.

—(2008) 'Evidence, the Conservative Paradigm, and School Choice', in W. Feinberg and C. Lubienski (eds), *School Choice Policies and Outcomes: Philosophical and Empirical Perspectives on Limits to Choice in Liberal Democracies* (Albany, NY: SUNY Press) pp. 61–78.

Howe, K. and Eisenhart, M. (2000) 'A Study of Boulder Valley School District's Open Enrollment System', at http://epicpolicy.org/publication/a-study-boulder-valley-school-districts-open-enrollment-program (accessed on 26 November 2009).

Johnson, L. (1965) 'Commencement Address at Howard University: "To Fulfill These Rights"', 4 June 1965, at http://www.hpol.org/lbj/civil-rights/ (accessed on 26 November 2009).

Karsten, S., Felix, C., Ledoux, G., Meijnen, W., Roeleveld, J. and Van Schooten, E. (2006) 'Choosing Segregation or Integration? The Extent and Effects of Ethnic Segregation in Dutch Cities', *Education and Urban Society* 38, 2: 228–47.

Lauder, H. and Hughs, D. (1999) *Trading in Futures: Why Markets in Education Don't Work* (Philadelphia, PA: Open University Press).

Lubienski, C. and Lubienski, S. (2006) *Charter, Private and Public Schools and Academic Achievement: New Evidence from NAEP Mathematics Data* (New York: National Center for the Study of Privatization in Education, Teachers College, Columbia University).

McNeil, L. (2000) *Contradictions of Control: Educational Costs of Standardization* (New York: Routledge).

McNeil, L., Coppola, E., Radigan, J. and Heilig, J. V. (2008) 'Avoidable Losses: High-Stakes Accountability and the Dropout Crisis', *Education Policy Analysis Archives* 16, 3, at http://epaa.asu.edu/epaa/v16n3/ (accessed on 26 November 2009).

National Center for Education Statistics, National Assessment of Educational Progress (2005) *The Nation's Report Card. America's Charter Schools: Results from the NAEP 2003 Pilot Study* (Washington, DC: NCES 2005-456).

National Commission on Educational Excellence (1983) *A Nation at Risk: The Imperative for Education Reform* (Washington, DC: Government Printing Office).

Orfield, G. and Lee, Chungmei (2006) *Racial Transformation and the Changing Nature of Segregation* (Cambridge, MA: The Civil Rights Project at Harvard University).

*Pierce v. Society of Sisters* (1925) 268 U.S. 510.

Reagan, Ronald (1983) 'Remarks on Receiving the Final Report of the National Commission on Excellence in Education', 26 April 1983, at http://www.reagan.utexas.edu/archives/speeches/1983/42683d.htm (accessed on 26 November 2009).

Robelson, E. (2008) 'NAEP Gap Continuing for Charters', *Education Week*, 19 May 2008, at www.wmich.edu/evalctr/charter (accessed on 26 November 2009).

Rothstein, R. (2004) *Class and Schools* (Washington, DC: Economic Policy Institute).

—(2008) 'Whose Problem is Poverty?' *Educational Leadership* 65, 7: 8–13.

Salamone, R. (1986) *Equal Education under the Law: Legal Rights and Federal Policy in the Post 'Brown' Era* (New York: St. Martin's Press).

Strike, K. (1985) 'Is There a Conflict between Equity and Excellence', *Educational Evaluation and Policy Analysis* 7, 4: 409–16.

Witte, J., Wolf, P. J., Cowen, J., Fleming, D. and Lucas-McLean, J. (2009) *The MPCP Longitudinal Educational Growth Study Second Year Report* (Fayetteville, AR: School Choice Demonstration Project), at http://www.uaedreform.org/SCDP/Milwaukee_Eval/Report_10.pdf (accessed on 26 November 2009).

# Moving from Educational Equality to Improving the Education of the Least Advantaged

James Tooley

## Chapter Outline

## Introduction

The more I read of Harry Brighouse on educational equality the less I understand why he is concerned with it, or even what he means by it. His current essay doesn't help. In this essay, I first explore Brighouse's implicit definition of educational equality. If the concept means more than a concern for the least advantaged, then it implies the possibility of very severe interventions in family life, as Brighouse recognizes. However, he believes that the principle of 'legitimate parental partiality' can save many of the features of family life that he sensibly holds dear. My argument is that it can't, at least not in the real world of policy prescriptions or even decisions about what parents can or cannot legitimately do. Indeed, given these difficulties I suggest that abandoning educational equality altogether and replacing it with a concern for the education of the least advantaged might be a more fruitful approach.

One of the policy areas that seems to have potential for helping the least advantaged concerns 'choice'; I explore Brighouse's difficulties with this concept and suggest that they are not substantial. I also suggest that his endorsement of formal choice systems such as targeted vouchers is along the right lines. But this implies an endorsement of a role for private education; I show how Brighouse's principle of parental partiality legitimizes use of private schools too, at least for many users both rich and poor.

Before I set out on this argument, however, let me stress that I'm arguing on the territory set by Brighouse. This is not territory in which I feel particularly comfortable, with its always benign state frequently and costlessly intervening to obstruct personal freedom when and where required. I find such ideas rather unpalatable, as my extended work elsewhere will make clear (see especially Tooley, 2000, 2008a, 2009). It's true that Brighouse and his collaborator, Adam Swift, write: 'Fundamental to the many varieties of liberalism is some version of the idea that individuals have rights to control over their own lives, rights that may not be overridden except, perhaps, when they conflict with those of others, or to avert very great disasters' (Brighouse and Swift, 2006b, p. 80); this definition seems fine to me, as they imply it is to them too. However, the ways in which these rights can potentially be overridden for Brighouse and Swift leaves me chilled – their benign state could potentially even ban the reading of bedtime stories to children under specified circumstances ('If it turned out that bedtime stories could be substituted by other, less equality-disrupting activities, and that banning them would result in no loss to the distinctive values that parents and children are able to derive from their relationship, then our account would have no grounds for objecting to their prevention' Brighouse and Swift, 2009, p. 69). I can't feel comfortable in such a world, which feels positively illiberal and uncomfortably like Nazi Germany, Soviet Russia or Maoist China. But anyway, let's see what progress we can make by moving on to Brighouse's territory, if only for the duration of this chapter.

## What is educational equality and why is it desirable?

In Brighouse's first section, he deploys 'a vague concept of educational equality, focusing mainly on unequal quality of resources in school' (p. 26). This is only by way of background introduction; his more substantial approach

> rests on an intuition about what it takes for a competition to be fair. . . . It is unfair, then, if some get a worse education than others because, through no fault of their own, this puts them at a disadvantage in the competition for these unequally distributed goods. (p. 27[1])

So educational inequality is about unfairness; educational equality presumably pertains when this unfairness is eliminated. He gives us two conceptions of how this might be achieved, the meritocratic and the radical. (It's odd to me that it's not clear from the essay which conception Brighouse endorses: surely this matters?) The *meritocratic* conception is where an 'individual's prospects for educational achievement *may* be a function of that individual's talent and effort, but it *should not* be influenced by her social class background' (p. 7, emphasis added). But this, he says, may seem to some 'insufficiently egalitarian' (p. 28). For, it neglects that talent too could be unfairly distributed as a result of social origin, hence the *radical* conception: 'An individual's prospects for educational achievement should be a function *neither of that individual's level of natural talent or* [*sic*] *social class background* but only of the *effort* she applies to education' (p. 29, emphasis added).

I genuinely don't see why he stops there. For there's enough evidence too that a child's propensity to make an effort can also be influenced by social class background as well as genes – indeed, Brighouse agrees with the former,[2] but for no apparent reason still decides 'effort' is worth insulating in his conception. He writes 'no one deserves the talents they were born with' (p. 29). I'd like to say instead, 'no one deserves the talents, *including the ability to make an effort,* they were born with'. Perhaps one danger of including 'effort' as well as 'talent' would be that it might lead us to wonder how the radical conception of educational equality could possibly be achieved. But in any case, this is already a problem, as Brighouse admits. He gives us an example of two families, featuring Ron Glum and Barbara Lyon. How would equalizing their educational achievement play out in practice? Brighouse says: 'Almost certainly it would require either neglecting Barbara in a way that would be emotionally damaging, or intervening in Ron's family in a way that would alienate him from his parents' (p. 32).

Indeed, he submits, to achieve the radical conception you might have to 'severely damage' some children, by, for instance, 'lobotomizing them' (p. 33). This, says Brighouse, 'would be seriously morally wrong' (p. 33). Too true. So we don't have to go that far: 'Educational equality is not as important as that . . . which is why the right [*inter alia* not to be lobotomized] presents a barrier to achieving educational equality' (p. 33).

However, for Brighouse, 'this does not mean that the radical conception fails to pick out a value that should be pursued as far as is permitted by the constraints imposed by other important values' (p. 33). Brighouse puts it schematically: if 'to achieve X you would have to violate Y', this doesn't mean that X doesn't matter: 'X might matter a lot, just not enough to justify violating value Y' (p. 33). This, he says 'helps to . . . refute' (p. 33) a common argument against the radical conception of educational equality. But does it really? Try some other Xs and Ys: for instance, I know a woman who would value having lots of boyfriends (X); however, she knows that this would cause her husband to be upset (Y). Her decision is to abandon X and concentrate on keeping her husband happy. Is there any sense in which we would want to say that X still matters to her? I would have thought it distinctly unhelpful (especially to her husband). No, she has *abandoned* X because it brings about Y. Even on this very simple level, I'm not convinced that Brighouse shouldn't consider abandoning his X (educational equality) because it could lead to such unfortunate consequences (lobotomizing children).

However, Brighouse clearly wants to keep the concept; no, we mustn't go so far as lobotomizing children, but this doesn't stop us doing as much as we can to bring about educational equality. He agrees, 'the barriers to achieving educational equality are enormous' (p. 31). But how can we go about it in practice? What Brighouse does accept, in principle, is that moving towards educational equality requires a two-pronged attack:

- First prong: focusing on the least advantaged, enhancing their educational environment somewhat;
- Second prong: focusing on the more advantaged, reducing their educational environment somewhat.

Both prongs of the attack are necessary. For with the first prong alone, then the concept of 'educational equality' reduces to 'benefiting the least advantaged'. As it happens this is one of the additional values that Brighouse recognizes is a possible challenge to 'educational equality', which is additional support to suggest that he agrees that the two-pronged approach in principle is required. But there's plenty of other evidence in his writings to support the notion that the two-pronged attack is necessary to move towards educational equality, as I'll outline in the next section.

# Middle-class families as barriers to educational equality

Brighouse quotes approvingly and at length from Richard Rothstein, who notes how it is precisely the contrasting family backgrounds of middle-class and poor children that lead to educational disadvantage (see the extended quote on p. 47). Moreover, Brighouse and his collaborator Swift note that there is a hugely important connection between 'certain parenting styles and subsequent economic advantage', noting with agreement one argument that 'middle class parenting styles are better than working-class ones at preparing children to negotiate their way through the complex institutions they will encounter as children' (Brighouse and Swift, 2006a, p. 489).

These bring (or indeed *are*, depending on your definition of education) educational advantages that would be exceedingly difficult to undermine by simply changing the *schooling* of the least advantaged. It can't be simply a question of spending 'considerably more *resources* . . . on educating children from lower socio-economic backgrounds than on children from more advantaged backgrounds, and that these resources be spent *effectively* ' (Brighouse, this volume, p. 28, emphasis added), as Brighouse says at one point in his current essay. When he outlines how such resources, efficiently spent, might compensate for family advantage in education, he's totally unconvincing:

> [T]o educate students who face the most barriers to achievement to the same level as those who face the fewest barriers takes more money and resources. Higher need students need better teacher: student ratios, they need extended school days and schooling during the summer which *replicates the enjoyable and casually educational experiences that upper-middle-class students get from expensive summer camps and spending time with their highly educated families and friendship networks.* (p. 51, emphasis added)

Is he serious, in the italicized passage, that compulsory schooling during the summer for disadvantaged kids could possibly replicate all those beautiful things experienced by the middle-class family relaxing on holiday? Who is he kidding? I think Brighouse's more sensible comment, reflecting on Rothstein's observations above, is 'The conclusion I draw from these observations is that there is something naïve in hoping that educational equality can be fully achieved through measures directed solely at schools' (p. 48). Agreed. And if it must be directed at families, then the two-pronged attack is necessary, to distinguish a concern from educational equality from that of simply concern for the less advantaged. Similarly, I agree with Brighouse's (and Swift's) admission that concentrating on schooling is unlikely to be a particularly powerful way of addressing educational inequality:

> Some strands in the egalitarian tradition have tended to assume . . . that *something close enough to fair equality of opportunity can be achieved through a combination of public education policies intended to marginalize the impact of expensive private schooling* . . . However, recent research in economics and sociology casts doubt on this assumption, suggesting that in fact parenting styles, and other factors integral to valuable familial relationships, may have as much if not more impact on prospects for income and wealth than transfers from parents to children. (Brighouse and Swift, 2009, p. 58).

That is, 'The family, even when kept within its genuinely valuable bounds, seems to be more threatening to the prospects for equality of opportunity, even of the conventional kind, than social democrats had hoped' (Brighouse and Swift, 2009, p. 59).

So if we're to move towards educational equality, then we're going to have to be involved in the two-pronged attack mentioned above; and this has to involve curbing advantaged families. Brighouse admits as much: 'Few people argue seriously that the USA's school system realizes any kind of ideal of educational equality. But what they do argue is that the measures that would be required to make it more equal would diminish parents' freedom to control their children's *education* as they see fit' (p. 34, emphasis added). And as he clearly acknowledges that education is broader than schooling, this has serious implications for advantaged families. But Brighouse believes there is a way around this, and that his principle of legitimate parental partiality protects families, at least like his. But is the principle as powerful as Brighouse hopes? I think it is fatally flawed as a basis for any policy prescriptions at all.

## The illegitimate self-indulgence of parental partiality

The family is of crucial importance to Brighouse (and his collaborator Swift) in giving rise to values that can legitimately undermine educational equality:

> We share the common view that familial relationships are valuable enough to make society A, in which people enjoy Rawlsian fair equality of opportunity but lack familial relationships, worse than society B, where there is a good deal of inequality of opportunity but plentiful family life. This means that parents should be permitted to engage in forms of partiality necessary for the realization of the most important familial relationship goods, and they would be justified in doing so, even where that would disrupt that version of equality of opportunity. (Brighouse and Swift, 2009, p. 50).

The notion of legitimate parental partiality is of huge importance to Brighouse (and Swift), because it sanctions many of the things that any family would want to indulge in, such as reading bedtime stories to children, taking their children on foreign holidays and to church, *even though manifestly these undermine educational equality*. The principle is, if you like, a partial protection against the second prong of the attack mentioned above. So what is legitimate parental partiality? Brighouse gives an outline on pp. 36–7 and points to other of his accounts for a fuller focus. The key points are that the particular interest that 'parents and children have in being able to have intimate relationships of deep connection with one another' leads to the legitimizing of partiality, such as 'reading bedtime stories to one's own children (and not, if one doesn't want to, to other people's)', even though this is 'at some cost to educational equality'.

When I first read this kind of account I thought (and wrote, see Tooley, 2000, 2008b): all very convenient for the likes of Brighouse (and Swift), whose family lives remain intact, whilst still enabling them to insist that, really, they are concerned with promoting educational equality (even though all their continuing efforts within their families continue to promote educational *in*equality). And this is so even though there seem to be urgent problems globally which might make their attitude smack of complacency. Perhaps I felt mean to have such thoughts. But now having delved deeper into Brighouse and Swift's writings, there seems to be an admission in their own voices that what I felt before was actually bang-on: For Brighouse and Swift concede that their discussion of 'legitimate parental partiality' is *not* aimed at explaining to any particular parent 'what she may legitimately do for her children' (Brighouse and Swift, 2009, p. 49). Nor, I suggest in the same spirit, could it be aimed at explaining to particular policy-makers what they might legitimately do for the families and children under their jurisdiction. For a full answer to those questions depends on knowledge of the context in which parents and policy-makers find themselves. So, 'in a world where some lack what they need for mere survival', Brighouse and Swift acknowledge that 'much of the time and energy spent by affluent parents on promoting the interests of their children' could be 'illegitimate self-indulgence' (ibid., p. 50): Indeed, 'in a world of that kind, much of the provision, for oneself and one's children, of those very familial relationship goods that our account hold crucial to human well-being similarly exceeds the bounds of legitimate partiality' (ibid.).

So their account raises the question

> how should we acknowledge the fact that parents acting to realize familial relationship goods for themselves and their children are

using resources in ways that do not merely deprive others of a fair chance of a good education and a good job, but could otherwise be deployed to provide opportunities for those very familial relationship goods to others who have least of them – or to provide food to the starving? *Our analysis is limited by our inability to provide a satisfactory treatment of these quite general and controversial issues.* (Brighouse and Swift, 2009, p. 51, emphasis added)

Their work here cannot 'offer any particular answers' (ibid.). To do that, one would have to go into the particulars of the situation – and clearly given what they've said here, they are aware that this means the global realities. Again: 'we explicitly left open the issue of the extent to which people should be free to pursue those goods, in their own and their children's lives, in circumstances where the conflict was with more urgent moral claims' (ibid., p. 62). Finally, just to make sure we have got this point: Parents are correct to 'feel self-indulgent' if they 'are giving disproportionate weight to the interests of their children in a world where others are starving' (ibid., p. 74).

Now, in the current essay under discussion, Brighouse is coming in from the philosophical cold to address real policies in the real world (unlike in the papers in the elite philosophy journals where the discussion remains on the abstract level). This real world is precisely one 'where others are starving' and millions of children are without any schooling at all. Indeed, he describes the terrible conditions in the USA for the poor (Brighouse seems rather self-satisfied that he has 'quite deliberately disregarded the preferences of some readers to be able to read only about the country they inhabit' (p. 17). But why should we be so excited about his prescriptions for educational 'socialism in two countries', the USA and the UK?). He knows that the developing world is much, much worse. So with this reality, the caveats from Brighouse and Swift state quite clearly that the principle of parental partiality as Brighouse wants to use it in the current essay is not valid. It really is complacent, illegitimate self-indulgence to raise the principle in defence of families like his, reading bedtime stories and taking the children on exotic holidays, when millions are starving and are out of school altogether.

So without the defence offered by the principle of legitimate parental partiality, the attack is justified against families like his, if we're concerned with moving towards educational equality. That's a pretty serious threat I would have thought. Perhaps this is why Brighouse concludes his discussion of values with: 'I think that the values of family life and of benefiting the least advantaged are more important than educational equality' (p. 44). And he outlines how important is the concern for the least advantaged:

> The basic idea here is that it really matters that social institutions should be designed to benefit those who have the lowest prospects for having a flourishing life. These include some people who have very severe disabilities, and also those who have the lowest incomes and lowest places in the occupational structure and status hierarchies of a society. (p. 41).

This seems like a more promising approach for social reformers like Brighouse. Focusing on the concept of educational equality, at least in the real world, as opposed to within the confines of learned journals, is far too fraught with dangers for liberals to consider. But dropping it as something desirable doesn't mean that we can't get on with helping the less advantaged, a value that both Brighouse and I seem to share.

One way I've written about helping the less advantaged is through educational choice (see Tooley, 2000, 2008a, 2009). This is one of four areas that Brighouse specifically considers as being amenable to reforms to help ameliorate educational inequality (the others are Admissions, Funding and Accountability). How does Brighouse see choice fitting into the picture?

## The virtues of choice

Brighouse does seem to prevaricate on whether or not he thinks choice is a good thing or not, on grounds of educational equality (which I suggest might now reduce to a concern for the less advantaged). First, he begins by noting that 'There is a very strong, and regrettable, tendency on the left to see choice as the enemy of equality and therefore to assume that choice should have no place in an egalitarian policy framework' (p. 54). However, this is explicitly because '*There is no school system without school choice, and those who oppose school choice typically ignore the massive, and unjust, significance of choice in the pre-existing system*' (p. 58). This is a very powerful point. In any system of school zoning, as predominates in many countries around the world, the presence of a good state school dramatically pushes up property prices, as Brighouse notes. So it is absolutely right that

> middle-class and wealthy parents who are unsatisfied with their children's schools have a choice. They can move to the neighbourhood within their district where most of the middle-class and wealthy children go. Or they can move to the suburbs, where their children's school will spend, in the USA, considerably more per pupil than an inner-city school. Thus do schools segregate by class . . . (p. 58)

Earlier he makes the same point:

> The neighbourhood schooling model was *already* a choice model, because people have choice over which neighbourhood they live in, and for many parents who are relatively advantaged one of the key factors they weigh in making this choice is neighbourhood school quality. In other words, though school choice is not direct, it is nevertheless built into the surrounding institutions. (p. 20)

Moreover, because of this factor, Brighouse notes that under zoning, one is able to obscure the fact of choice unlike in more explicit school-choice programmes:

> [W]hereas in direct school choice systems there is some transparency, and the parents of more advantaged children cannot collude to exclude less advantaged children from the desired school, in the neighbourhood choice model they do exclude less advantaged

children by driving up the value of housing within the catchment area boundaries of a 'good' school making attendance unafford-able for less advantaged parents. (p. 21)

So there is a charge of hypocrisy here (using the term unsparingly used by Swift) against any one on the left who would be against choice, if they don't recognize that they are also beneficiaries of choice systems by virtue of where they have chosen to base their families.

However, what of formal school choice systems proper? Brighouse has a number of criticisms of educational markets which seem to illuminate a number of misunderstandings of the ways markets work – or perhaps show Brighouse only able to entertain ideas on markets in education within the narrow context of the status quo rather than thinking imaginatively about how they could manifest themselves if given free rein. Here I'll only be able to point briefly to some issues, based on my more detailed accounts elsewhere (especially Tooley, 2000 and 2008a).

First, Brighouse considers competition and quality:

The purpose of choice in the provision of public services is to trigger competition which is, in turn, supposed to improve performance of the competing units. In order for choice to have the benefits claimed for it with respect to quality it must have the side effect of compro-mising equality; if it did not then it could not yield the efficiency gains that purportedly justify it. If choice is going to be used to improve provision of these services it must be because better providers are chosen by more people. Those who choose the worse providers get worse provision. The better and worse providers have to compete. *Over time* this should produce improvement (if markets work as their enthusiasts claim). But *at any given time* there will be better and worse providers – those who have the worse providers are worse off (in one relevant respect) than those who have the better providers. (pp. 54–5)

But this general description of competition applies to any markets, not just school markets. It's true of supermarkets and airlines, to name two that I've used over the last few days. The point that Brighouse fails to note is that, in general, in any mature market competition keeps standards overall high. In the type of pretend-markets that he's aware of in schools in the United Kingdom, for instance, the danger of 'sink' schools is ever present and real. It's simply not true in mature markets elsewhere, where firms go out of business or change ownership long before they get to such a state of inadequacy. It may be true that British Airways is better than KLM (say), but this doesn't mean that if I choose to fly KLM I'm going to be dumped in France en route to West Africa. Not at all; competition in the market makes sure that all airlines competing on these same routes offer a roughly similarly desirable service. The same goes for supermarkets. Tesco may be better than Sainsbury's (say), but if I go to either I'll know that the food I buy will definitely not give me food poisoning. And there's no reason, as I've argued elsewhere that genuine markets in education wouldn't have the same features, rather than featuring the levels of inadequacy of sink schools you get in current state systems.

Brighouse thinks that there are substantial reasons why markets in education may be different; he writes:

> In fact there are reasons to be sceptical that choice will yield substantial efficiency benefits in schooling. Enthusiasts for school choice tend to overestimate the quality of information that parents have, and to underestimate (or even ignore) the transaction costs consumers face, and the power that producers have in educational markets. They tend to assume, in other words, that markets in schooling can be *more perfect* than they really can be. (p. 55, emphasis added)

If it's a defence of 'perfect' markets he's after, then he won't get one from me. I'm firmly in the classical liberal tradition of Adam Smith and Hayek that all markets are imperfect; indeed, one of the virtues of markets is precisely that they constitute a *discovery mechanism in an imperfect world*, including one of imperfect information (see Seldon, 1990 and references to my work above). Perfect markets – with perfect competition and perfect information – are a construct of mathematical economists for their abstract models, which may or may not have purchase in the real world. I don't know from where Brighouse gets this misunderstanding, but note that it is a common one from those who are sceptical about markets in education.

But let's have a look at the particular sources of Brighouse's unease. First, there's the quality of information available to parents. He mentions UK government tables of test results: but from my perspective, while his conclusions about them seem correct, these are not market-driven information, but are imposed government bureaucracy. Indeed, as he says, and I agree, it is not even clear 'that even good value-added tables give many parents relevant information' (p. 56). But that is not the information that parents and students are looking at in a real market. 'Some of' the information that parents are seeking, agrees Brighouse, 'can be gleaned through informal means' (p. 57), but 'much of it is simply not available at all' (p. 57). The first point is important, pointing to one of the ways in a genuine market that people can glean information. I've just returned from China, where I was involved in parents' meetings at low-cost private schools serving poor migrant workers to Beijing. The range of informal information the parents brought to bear was rather impressive I thought. They were worried about staff volatility – about teachers who had moved in and out of the school over the past term. They were worried that not enough emphasis was being placed on the arts and sports. Some were concerned about the low quality of food from the kitchen, others about the floors in certain classrooms and the low quality of infrastructure in general. And then there were particular complaints about individual pupils – one couldn't do his summer homework, for instance, because he hadn't been taught all the subject, said his mother. And all this – and more – information has been picked up by busy, largely illiterate parents who have gleaned it from their children and neighbours.

Other methods of gaining information include checking of brand reputations, studying consumer guides and focusing on price, a key part of information available in the market. Crucially, one of the virtues of markets is that not everyone has to be au fait with the available information – as long as some consumers are, and there is competition amongst suppliers, it is in the interest of the producer to assume that you are one of the informed customers and that you'll exercise your right of exit, and hence deprive him of business, if you are not satisfied with the quality of provision.

But the second point is perhaps a more important concession: If much of the type of information that Brighouse thinks important is 'not available at all', then doesn't this damn any alternatives to choice too? Brighouse notes that what demanding parents really want to know is 'not how good the school is, but how high the probability is that it will be good for *one's own child*' (p. 56). That certainly seems right. And this is where he suggests such information will not be available at all. But if there is no information available, then government planners will also not have any (relevant) information, and so will make choices for your child irrespective of what is good for him or her. Why is that any better? (Curiously, I see that Brighouse tries to have it both ways when he later writes under the title of accountability: 'educators at every level need good information in order to meet the challenge that the educational egalitarian sets them, and that includes information about how well children are performing at the low end of the achievement spectrum, and about who, exactly, those children are' (p. 62). If it's possible to gain such information for educational planners, then it's possible too for parents. My intuition is that he's probably right in saying that much of the information is simply impossible to gain centrally. This doesn't stop it existing as *tacit* knowledge in the market place, however; see Sowell, 1980.

What proponents of real choice in education ask is: in the face of imperfect information (that both Brighouse and I seem to suggest will be the most that is available) which would be the most preferable way of reaching high-quality education? I've argued elsewhere that choice in a competitive system would be, precisely because it capitalizes on the limited and tacit information that is available in a way that central planners cannot possibly do. In other words, you can't use an accusation of limited information to condemn choice systems: it's one of their virtues that they can deal better with limited information than the alternatives.

Brighouse then turns to transaction costs. He writes: 'These are also high for parents, and, to make matters worse, they are borne by children' (p. 57). The frustration for this commentator is that the limitations he lists are probably true for the systems of schooling as they stand now in the USA and the UK. But are they necessary features of educational systems, particularly those featuring genuine choice? Again, I've argued elsewhere that genuine markets in education are not likely to depend so entirely on such archaic institutions as schools, which do have these high transaction costs, but are likely to feature much more flexible means of delivering education (Tooley, 2000, 2005). So real educational markets are likely to exhibit features much closer to the 'trivial transaction costs involved in frequent changes in one's chosen brand of breakfast cereal' (p. 57) noted by Brighouse.

However, there is important new evidence available now from embryonic markets we see in developing countries. In the slums and shanty towns of Asia and Africa, poor people are abandoning public schooling *en masse*. They're appalled by its low standards. Instead, they're sending their children to low-cost private schools that are burgeoning in some of the poorest places on this planet. For the last decade I've been on an extraordinary journey across sub-Saharan Africa, India and China. I've been cataloguing and, more recently, assisting in the development of low-cost private schools. For anyone interested in how the poor are learning to help themselves, it is a wonderfully uplifting story. In slums and shanty towns around the developing world, the majority of poor school children – around 65–75 per cent – are attending low-cost private schools, affordable even to parents on minimum wages. Entrepreneurs have set up these schools against the odds; testing 24,000 children my researchers have shown that children in these low-cost private schools significantly outperform those in state schools, even after controlling for all relevant variables and the school-choice process, all for considerably lower cost than public education. (For more details see Tooley and Dixon, 2006; Tooley, 2009.)

In these embryonic markets, it's not clear that Brighouse's criticisms currently apply. For instance, in these markets it is simply not true that 'Schools must be above a certain size to be viable, so supply is inevitably restricted' (p. 57). In fact, schools can be very small in these more authentic markets, sometimes fewer than 100 students, perhaps because parents value a small school close to their home. Moreover, it's also not true that 'Any particular consumer has at most five or six schools that are realistic for them to use' (p. 57). In Kishanbagh, in Hyderabad, India, where I've been living the past two years, there are 34 schools, ranging in size from 80 to 1,800 children, all within reach of a child who lives in this area and walks or takes a short autorickshaw ride to the school. In Bortianor, Ghana, where I'm managing a small project, there are also about 20 private schools in the village, mostly with below 200 students, plus a government school, all similarly within reach of children from the village. Neither of these is atypical of the kinds of opportunities available in poor communities across developing countries. And parents at the meetings in Beijing will move their children to another school if they think nothing is being done about their complaints. So again, I don't think transaction costs can be used as a strong argument against choice in education.

This discussion of the problems of choice notwithstanding, it is interesting that Brighouse concludes his comments with the following rather up-beat assessment: *some* formal proposals for choice, he writes, such as those which 'target vouchers to children from low-income homes' have the 'real potential for being more egalitarian than the pre-existing *status quo*' (p. 59). So in other words, he can see that some choice programmes, correctly designed, can be better for educational equality than non-choice programmes. Indeed, there is considerable evidence accumulating showing that programmes such as targeted vouchers, and even universal vouchers, are beneficial both in terms of raising educational achievement, and doing this in a more equitable way than the alternatives.

The *universal* voucher scheme in Sweden came about through reforms in 1991 and 1992, which established 'the right of any nongovernment school that fulfils certain basic requirements to receive public funding on terms equal to those of public schools' (Sandström and Bergstrom, 2005, p. 23). The 'equal' funding is calculated at 85 per cent of the calculated average cost per student in the municipal schools, with the other 15 per cent accounting for overhead and administration of the municipalities. The figure was reduced to 75 per cent in 1995. Enrolment rules were also opened within the public sector, with money following pupils to public schools in other municipalities. As long as schools satisfy the National Agency for Education (NAE) that they are meeting certain quality requirements, including a general curriculum framework, and that they are non-discriminatory, *any* kind of school is eligible, from religious schools to schools run by for-profit corporations. However, no schools are allowed to charge tuition fees. Municipalities are allowed to say whether they consider the establishment of a new independent school would be harmful to existing schools, and their views must be taken into account by the NAE. Importantly, however, they have no veto on this, and must, by law, finance any independent school that has been approved by the NAE, which has on occasion approved schools against the municipality's will.

A rapid growth of independent schools has been experienced since reforms were introduced, although this differs between municipalities (in Sweden, schooling is primarily the responsibility of the municipalities, the lowest tier of government). Overall, only about 6 per cent of children of compulsory school age are in private schools, though this ranges from zero to nearly 20 per cent in some municipalities, with about 10 per cent in Stockholm. Significantly, more than half of the private schools are owned by limited liability companies, with several companies now running 'chains' of for-profit schools. One of these is Kunskapsskolan (which translates as 'The Knowledge School'). This company currently operates more than 20 schools, with about 6000 pupils. Other examples include the 'International English School', first opened in Stockholm in 1993, with now six schools across the country, and Pysslingen (with 12 schools) and Vittra (with 25 schools).

The voucher programmes in America, operating in 11 states and Washington DC, are all *targeted* voucher schemes, aimed at specific groups of children, such as those in low-income families, those with special needs, or those in failing (public) schools. For instance, the Milwaukee publicly funded voucher scheme – the Milwaukee Parent Choice Program (MPCP) – was introduced in 1990, specifically targeting low-income families to allow them to attend registered private schools. The voucher's value is set at the per-student subsidy rate provided to the government schools by the state. Parents qualify for a voucher only if their family income is no more than 1.75 times the official poverty level. In 1995 the programme was expanded, allowing around 15,000 students to participate. In 1998 the growth of the programme burgeoned, when the Wisconsin Supreme Court ruled that religious schools could participate in the programme, a decision endorsed by the US Supreme Court in 2002.

Other targeted voucher schemes occur in developing countries. In Colombia, a targeted voucher system was introduced in 1992, aimed at providing wider access to private education for poor students, inspired by the realization that there was a shortage of places offered by state secondary schools. The proposal allowed poor children to benefit from private school provision, moving out of the overcrowded public sector. Importantly, the private schools taking part offer an educational service that had been estimated to be of comparable quality to that found in government schools, but the typical cost of sending a pupil to private school, via the voucher scheme, is around *two-thirds* of the per-pupil cost of sending him to a government school. By 1997 more than 100,000 students from very low-income families had received subsidies through the programme.

Concerning the performance of these systems, these seem to be some widely accepted results:

- These approaches raise standards in education, better than standard approaches, often at a lower cost.
- The approaches are more equitable, helping extend access and opportunity to the most disadvantaged in society, better than standard alternatives.

First on *standards*: The evidence on voucher schemes is strong. Targeted vouchers succeed in raising the achievement levels of poor families, over and above what would normally be expected of them. There have been three major evaluations of the Milwaukee programme, for instance. Each concluded that 'choice has at least some significant benefits for its participants', while none finds that choice harms students: 'This is about as close as one gets to a positive consensus among researchers examining a controversial policy' (Greene, 2000). Some research has found quite dramatic increases. In Milwaukee, for instance, voucher students enrolled in private schools for three or more years performed substantially better, on average, than a control group of state school students, measured by standardized test scores (Greene et al., 1996). Even those less enthusiastic about the achievement increases concede that improvement is taking place: While scores always remain 'below national norms', the disadvantaged students enrolled on the voucher programme do not see their scores 'substantially decline as the students enter higher grades' – which would be the normal pattern, where 'inner-city student average scores decline relative to national norms in higher grades' (Witte, 1999, pp. 236–7).

Competition from the private sector also helps improve standards in state schools. In the universal voucher system of Sweden, research has found that competition from independent schools improves test results and final grades in the state schools. The higher the proportion of students in private schools, when controlled for the normal factors, the higher the grades in the state schools (Sandström and Bergstrom, 2002).

Second, on *equity:* Evidence unequivocally shows that targeted vouchers reach the intended disadvantaged families. Dr John Witte summarized the impact of the MPCP as targeting 'exactly the types of families that should have access to an alternative source of education' (Witte, 2000). In Milwaukee, the average income of families participating in the programme was $10,860, with 76 per cent of choice students from single, female-headed households. The standardized tests of choice students before they began in private school showed that they averaged below the 31st percentile. African American students made up 73 per cent of those enrolling in the programme between 1990 and 1994, while Hispanic students accounted for 21 per cent in the same period (Greene, 2000). Similarly, the Cleveland scheme also has been found to 'effectively serve' the population of families and children 'for which it was intended and developed'. In Cleveland 70 per cent of participating students were from single, female-headed households (Greene, 2000).

Concerning the universal voucher system in Sweden, research has also shown that the worse the state schools perform, the larger is the proportion of students attending private schools. In other words, there is no evidence that 'independent schools are more likely to be established in municipalities with "easy customers"', but rather that they are established often to serve disadvantaged young people (Sandström and Bergstrom, 2002, p. 23). Moreover, there is no evidence that 'low-achievers are adversely affected by increased competition from independent schools' (ibid., p. 26).

All this evidence suggests that Brighouse may be right when he concedes that some choice programmes, such as those with targeted or universal vouchers, could enhance educational equality (and a fortiori, concern for the less advantaged) more than non-choice arrangements.

Obviously much remains on the practical, empirical level to explore what kinds of choice programmes these could be, and I commend efforts to this end (see Tooley, 2008a for more discussion). But for the purposes of this essay I want to note two points: First, I suspect that his observations in favour of voucher type programmes will be met with disapproval by many of his (more?) egalitarian colleagues. And they'll be met thus because he seems to be endorsing a role for *private* education as a way of serving the least advantaged (for targeted voucher programmes are precisely those which allow poor families to use private schools if they prefer). This is not part of the armoury of many egalitarians.

Second, I observed above that any application of Brighouse's philosophical work to policy comes up against the very real problems in the real world (in Brighouse and Swift's own terms); however, it's worth stressing again that, in practice, the way that many of the world's poorest families respond to the educational poverty of state provision, is by sending their children to low-cost private schools, that is, by exercising choice within a schooling system (see Tooley and Dixon, 2006; Tooley, 2009). It would seem that in situations of real educational poverty in developing countries, parents seem to be agreeing with Brighouse – indeed, going even further – that choice is indeed the way forward to improve their conditions. Again, however, the choices of the poor are usually criticized by academic commentators and development experts, because they involve choices of private schools, and private schools are not part of the armoury of the experts to move towards education for the least advantaged (see, for instance, UNDP, 2003 and World Bank, 2003).

I wonder whether Brighouse would be able to justify this legitimization of private education within his own framework?

On the face of it, this idea seems unpromising. For Brighouse has written in many places against private schools, in this current essay and in earlier writings. However, observe that the accusation seems now usually to be against *elite* private schools, rather than *any* type of private schools – a point made clear by his collaborator Swift revising his argument of *How Not To Be a Hypocrite* (Swift, 2003): 'When I write of private schools, think of expensive elite private schools. It is the unfairness, not the privateness, with which my arguments will be concerned' (Swift, 2004, p. 9). So it may be that Brighouse could also justify low-cost private schools, or the poor using private schools through vouchers, as part of any acceptable reform scenario.

However, I believe we can go further than this. There seems to be some kernel of defence of private education within his (and Swift's) argument for legitimate parental partiality that can lead to a stronger defence of private education, both for the rich as well as the poor. Of course, how much this then has any bearing in reality is an open discussion, open to the same caveats we noted above when we move from philosophical to real worlds. But I think it's important to note that on a philosophical level, the principle of legitimate parental partiality is far more permissive than Brighouse and Swift seem to want it to be. (Perhaps this final section can be read in one of two ways: first, as an attempt at a philosophical justification for private education, using the territory set by Brighouse and Swift. Or alternatively, as additional ammunition for the argument against educational equality. For as soon as you focus on educational equality as an aim, then you have to invoke the principle of legitimate parental partiality as a defence against repressive regimes interfering in the bedrooms and holiday plans of the middle classes. But the principle of legitimate parental partiality is a pretty slippery beast, pretty permissive in all it allows. Perhaps best to drop it all together. We'll need to drop a focus on educational equality as a result. But that still leaves much good work to be done by focusing on the less advantaged.)

## The permissiveness of legitimate parental partiality

Schematically we can suppose there are four types of people who are motivated to send their children to private schools. Three of these have been catalogued by Brighouse and Swift:

First, there are those people whose family traditions are imbued with private school enrolment. Grandfather and father went to Eton, this is a family tradition that is of great importance for young Johnny to continue (Brighouse and Swift, 2009, p. 66).

Second, there are those who believe that only in a particular private school will their children get the best education for their particular specialized talents, whether these be sporting, academic, musical or whatever: 'Some send their children to elite private schools with no intention to confer competitive advantage but simply because they want them to have access to a world of particular excellences that they judge not otherwise, or at least not so readily available' (Brighouse and Swift, 2009, pp. 59–60).

Third, there are those who can't really pretend either of the above applies, who know they should be sending their children to state schools, but they want private education because they're weak-willed hypocrites. They're the kind of people addressed, it will come as no surprise, in the book by Brighouse's collaborator, *How Not To Be a Hypocrite* (Swift, 2003).

But there is a fourth category of people, not addressed by Brighouse or Swift, who should also get a look in here. These are those families who believe in self-reliance and self-help, for whom the very notion of sending their child to a school provided by the state would be as alien as putting their child on welfare for food or clothing. Now clearly, given the prevalence of almost universal state schooling provision, those families may be hard to find nowadays in the UK and the USA – although many of the two million families home-schooling their children in the USA probably fit into this category. My guess is that it's one of the motivations of families using private education in developing countries that I've catalogued elsewhere. But it was very likely a prevalent attitude amongst families, rich and poor, before or during the early imposition of state education in the UK and the USA: For instance, while writing this essay, I've been reading a biography of Arthur Seldon, the first editorial director of the Institute of Economic Affairs (Robinson, 2009). Arthur was raised by his adopted parents in a family 'which was typical in many ways of the "respectable working class" of that time . . . Hard work and help for other members of the community were accepted norms of behaviour and education was respected' (ibid., p. 13). One of the areas of 'self-help' valued within these kinds of communities was the ability to use (private) schools of their choice. Indeed, in the adoption agreement that Arthur's adoptive parents sign, the father 'undertakes *at his own expense to give the infant a thoroughly good education*' (ibid., p. 151, emphasis added).

What I contend is that Brighouse (and Swift) actually say that the principle of legitimate parental partiality allows (at least under many circumstances) parents in the first two categories to send their children to private school. I also contend that, had they thought of the fourth category of parent, the principle allows them too to use private education. The only parents who wouldn't be thus permitted under the principle are those in category three.

How do I arrive at this? First, consider my category four above. In defence of their principle of parental partiality, Brighouse and Swift argue: 'Without substantial opportunity to share himself intimately with his child, *in ways that reflect his own judgements about what is valuable*, the parent is deprived of the ability to forge and maintain an intimate relationship, and the child is deprived of that relationship' (Brighouse and Swift, 2009, p. 57, emphasis added). Moreover, 'What parents fundamentally have a right to is an intimate relationship of a certain kind with their children. . . . Parents have a right to determine whether the child will attend a church, a mosque, or neither; they have the right to . . . *share their enthusiasms regarding their own particular cultural heritage*' (Brighouse and Swift, 2006b, p. 102, emphasis added). I contend that for the particular kind of parent included in my fourth category above, the choice of private school precisely reflects the parents' 'judgements about what is valuable' and their 'own particular cultural heritage', and hence would be legitimized under the principle of parental partiality. Regarding Arthur Seldon's upbringing, for instance, Robinson quotes Beatrice Webb, the leading Fabian socialist emphasizing how much the emphasis on 'voluntary action', including independent education, was part of the cultural heritage of these 'respectable working class' communities in the East End of London: 'it is easy to overlook the influence for good of self-creating, self-supporting and self-governing communities; small enough to generate public opinion and the practical supervision of private morals, and large enough to stimulate charity, worship and study by communion and example' (quoted in Robinson, 2009, p. 46). Similarly, quoting Gertrude Himmelfarb, in the kind of community that Arthur was brought up in, 'individuals were encouraged to be responsible, self-reliant, and self-disciplined, . . . where those values were expressed in their relations to their family, their community, their religion, and, not least, their work' (quoted in Robinson, 2009, p. 49). In these communities – and, by extension, similar communities who use private (or home-) schooling today in developed and developing countries, or those who might seek to do so in some other world which we can explore philosophically – the choice of private education seems entirely acceptable under Brighouse's and Swift's discussion of legitimate parental partiality.

But the principle of parental partiality is even more permissive than this, I contend, legitimizing parents in both our first and second categories too. Concerning parents in both these categories, Brighouse and Swift write:

> [T]here can also be more specific contexts in which instances of . . . educational investment . . . are particularly valuable instantiations of the parent-child relationship . . . some parents wish their children to receive particular kinds of education neither because they want

> them to enjoy competitive advantage over others nor because they
> want them to partake of excellences that will make their lives go
> better in some general sense, but because the parent-child relation-
> ship itself, or perhaps the child's sense of herself as a member of a
> particular familial tradition, depends on the child's knowing or
> understanding particular things (cricket, classical languages, music)
> not otherwise available, or, perhaps, on the child attending the
> school that one of his parents and, maybe, one of his grandparents,
> attended. In such cases, familial relationship goods might indeed be
> invoked as grounds for permitting such . . . educational choices.
> (Brighouse and Swift, 2009, pp. 66–7)

Or on the first category alone, sending a child to private school
because of the standards of excellence required within: 'Sometimes
those excellences are themselves desired partly because of the role
that they will play in fostering and sustaining a close relationship
between parent and child' (Brighouse and Swift, 2009, pp. 59–60).
With these conditions satisfied, parents in our first and second
category would, it seems, be able to send their children to private
school under the principle of parental partiality.

Brighouse and Swift explore reasons why such instances might
not actually come under the rubric of legitimate parental partiality; in the three articles reviewed here the ducking and diving of
their argument is spread over around 100 pages, so it's not possible
to explore every nuance in the confined space at my disposal here;
nevertheless, I don't think I'm doing them any injustices by noting
that in the end they concede:

> Doubtless there are families for whom . . . children's learning a
> particular accomplishment or attending a particular school, *are
> indeed means by which important familial relationship goods
> are realized. Were permitting such interactions the only way for
> families to realize those goods, that would indeed be a weighty
> consideration in favour of their protection.* (Brighouse and Swift,
> 2009, pp. 68–9, emphasis added)

It's true, they do add, in a further twist, 'Typically, however, there
are, or can easily be, alternative mechanisms for their realization,

mechanisms that conflict less with other valuable distributive goals, so the case for their protection is weak' (ibid., p. 69), but it's this caveat that seems weak to me, not the protection. For our first category this is obvious: it's precisely and only the particular school itself that matters to preserve the family traditions: great grandmother, grandmother and mother all went to Colston Girls' School, so daughter wants to go there too. Sending her instead to the local comprehensive is precisely *not* fulfilling the family tradition.

For our second category it's slightly more complex, but nonetheless the difficulties it raises are also the difficulties raised for Brighouse and Swift when they want to defend their bedtime stories, foreign holidays and church attendance. For a start, our second category consists of parents who are telling us that they believe it is only in this particular private school that their child's particular musical, sporting or whatever talents will be realized and that this realization is something important for their familial relationships. I suppose Brighouse could allow the authorities[3] to question both these parental motives and also whether or not there could be alternative mechanisms for the fulfilment of the childhood talents, whilst still keeping the family bond alive. But herein lie severe dangers. For exactly the same questioning, by the same authorities, could be raised about Brighouse and Swift's treasured family activities too: indeed, Brighouse and Swift agree that 'Some parents read their children bedtime stories precisely in order to give them a competitive edge' (Brighouse and Swift, 2009, p. 60), which would then not allow them to plead legitimate parental partiality. 'So Dr Brighouse', the inspectors might ask: 'you read your children bedtime stories. You're doing this just to give them competitive advantage, no?' How is he going to prove that his motives are sound? I don't believe he could. Requiring such a defence of parental motivation seems dangerous territory for any liberal moral philosophy to intrude on.

Similarly, how can we – or the appropriate authorities – prove that there are 'alternative mechanisms' for the realization of the childhood needs and parental bonds, against parental protests that these alternatives are not the same at all? A parallel question is raised about Brighouse's bedtime stories too. Boldly, as we've already noted in a different context, Brighouse and Swift have conceded:

> If it turned out that bedtime stories could be substituted by other, less equality-disrupting activities, and that banning them would result in no loss to the distinctive values that parents and children are able to derive from their relationship, then our account would have no grounds for objecting to their prevention. (Brighouse and Swift, 2009, p. 69)

My guess is that they're putting themselves on the line here because they really do believe they could convince whoever they had to convince that the bedtime story substitutes were really not the same for their family relationships. I argue that any case that depends upon parents having to justify such intimate choices reflecting family values – whether of bedroom activities or private school choice– is moving into dangerous and illiberal territory.

My suggestion is that categories one to four cover all parents who use private schools. If so, the only people who aren't justified in sending their children to private school, in terms of Brighouse and Swift's legitimate parental partiality, are those unfortunate parents in category three. Everyone else is justified. (However, even for category three people, help is at hand. They could read my discussion of *How Not To Be a Hypocrite* in Tooley, 2008b and 2009; you never know, they might be persuaded to come into the fold of the first, second or fourth categories.)

Before we conclude this section, it is worth noting in passing that Brighouse also sees another way in which private education might be morally justified: if it plays its part in benefiting the least advantaged. He makes this point on p. 42 in his current essay. And he (and Swift) elaborate it further elsewhere:

> One argument for permitting elitist private education, and thereby allowing parents who can afford it to buy their children an unfairly good chance of getting a well-rewarded and interesting job, is that

preventing their doing so may have damaging incentive effects – where 'damaging' means 'deleterious to the interests of the worse off'. Deprived of this means of investing in their children's well-being, they will have less interest in being productive, choose more leisure or consumption and less work, producing economic inefficiency and harming economic growth. It is likely also that some of what they would choose to invest in their children is itself productive, not only in helping them achieve well-rewarded positions but in terms of helping to produce goods that accrue to the worse off. . . . if an unfair or unequal competition helps the worse off, all things considered, fairness considerations do not seem very weighty. (Brighouse and Swift, 2006a, p. 485)

There is no space to explore whether such conditions pertain in the real world. Nevertheless, it's clear that on a number of grounds, support of private education fits, or potentially fits, perfectly comfortable within Brighouse's philosophical framework.

## Conclusions

Brighouse's educational equality seems a particularly fraught concept. From his own definition, it is clear that there is an intimate link with the family. So a pursuit of educational equality is bound to come into conflict with family values. Brighouse thinks he can protect many of the precious things about family life by recourse to the principle of legitimate parental partiality which he has hatched with his collaborator Adam Swift. I've explored this and suggested that this simply isn't the case, once you move to actual family choices or policy prescriptions in the real world. Defending parental partiality really is an exercise in frivolous self-indulgence, in a world where people are starving and many children are not in school at all.

However, rather than use this to dismiss his policy proposals altogether, I suggest that some of the discussion raises valuable points. Of particular interest to me is Brighouse's discussion of choice. If we can get around the idea that markets somehow have to be perfect (a predilection of mathematical economists somehow adopted by Brighouse) then we can avoid the problems he raises about information in the market; likewise his problems with transaction costs are avoidable once one considers the potential for more authentic educational markets rather than the status quo of monopoly state provision considered by Brighouse. Significantly, Brighouse points to the hypocrisy amongst those egalitarians who condemn choice, while avoiding the fact that their ability to select a family home location reveals the inevitability (and unfairness) of choice within any state schooling system. Finally, and importantly, Brighouse suggests that formal choice systems including targeted vouchers might well be more egalitarian than current state schooling systems.

But won't this defence come up against Brighouse's own disavowal of private education? By delving deep into Brighouse's and Swift's discussion of legitimate parental partiality applied to the four types of parent who are likely to use private education, I suggest not. The principle permits many parents to use private education, and any attack on this privilege is equally, it would appear, an attack on the privilege of bedtime story-reading and other middle-class delights. Private education can, after all, be part of the armoury of liberal philosophers like Brighouse and Swift.

Brighouse writes: 'I think that the values of family life and of benefiting the least advantaged are more important than educational equality' (p. 44). Agreed. I wish then that he could be persuaded to drop his interest altogether in educational equality, and to focus on these other two values he finds more desirable. It's a very potent combination, the strength of the family coupled with concern for the least advantaged. Focusing on those two alone could lead us to some pretty helpful policy reforms – including exploration of targeted and universal vouchers, and reforms to help strengthen the poor's use of low-cost private education. An unhelpful obsession with educational equality instead seems to lead us up a garden path of counter-intuitive and illiberal philosophical meanderings.

## Notes

1. [Where no reference is given, this is to Brighouse (2009) in this volume].
2. 'If it is unfair for a child's prospects for achievement to be influenced by her social origins, why it is fair for them to be influenced by her natural talent (which is entirely beyond her control) or level of effort (which is itself heavily influenced by familial and neighbourhood factors)?' (p. 28).
3. I've put it in these terms to make clear that some state authorities would have to be adjudicating on these issues for them to make any sense – Brighouse and Swift use the term 'permissions' in several places in this respect.

## References

Brighouse, Harry and Swift, Adam (2006a) 'Equality, Priority, and Positional Goods', *Ethics* 116, (April): 471–97.

—(2006b) 'Parents' Rights and the Value of the Family', *Ethics* 117, (October): 80–108.

—(2009) 'Legitimate Parental Partiality', *Philosophy and Public Affairs* 37, 1: 43–80.

Greene, J. P. (2001) *An Evaluation of the Florida A-Plus Accountability and School Choice Program* (New York: Center for Civic Innovation).

Greene, J. P., Peterson, P. E., Du, J. with Boeger, L., and Frazier, C. (1996) 'The Effectiveness of School Choice in Milwaukee: A Secondary Analysis of Data from the Program's Evaluation', *Program in Education Policy and Governance*, Occasional Paper 96-3, Harvard University.

Robinson, Colin (2009) *Arthur Seldon: A Life for Liberty* (London: Profile Books).

Sandström, F. Mikael and Bergstrom, Fredrik (2002) *School Vouchers in Practice: Competition Won't Hurt You!*, The Research Institute of Industrial Economics, Working Paper No. 578, Stockholm, Sweden, 30 April 2002.

—(2005) 'School Vouchers in Practice: Competition Will Not Hurt You!' *Journal of Public Economics*, 89: 351–80.

Seldon, Arthur (1990) *Capitalism* (Oxford: Basil Blackwell).

Sowell, Thomas (1980) *Knowledge and Decisions* (New York: Basic Books).

Swift, Adam (2003), *How Not To Be a Hypocrite: School Choice for the Morally Perplexed Parent* (London and New York: Routledge).

—(2004) 'The Morality of School Choice', *Theory and Research in Education* 2, 1: 7–21.

Tooley, James (2005) 'Education Reclaimed', in Booth, P (ed.) *Towards a Liberal Utopia?* (London: Profile Books).

—(2008a) *E.G. West: Economic Liberalism and the Role of Government in Education* (New York and London: Continuum (Continuum Library of Educational Thought)).

—(2008b) 'From Adam Swift to Adam Smith: How the "Invisible Hand" overcomes Middle Class Hypocrisy', *Journal of Philosophy of Education* 41, 4: 727–41.

—(2009) *The Beautiful Tree: A Personal Journey into How the World's Poorest People Are Educating Themselves* (New Delhi: Penguin).

Tooley, James and Dixon, Pauline (2006) ' "*De Facto*" Privatisation of Education and the Poor: Implications of a Study from Sub-Saharan Africa and India', *Compare* 36, 4: 443–62.

UNDP (United Nations Development Program) (2003) *Human Development Report 2003* (New York: UNDP).

Witte, J. F. (1996) 'Who Benefits from the Milwaukee Choice Program?' in Fuller, B. and Elmore, R. with Orfield, G (eds) *Who Chooses? Who Looses? Culture, Institutions and the Unequal Effects of School Choice* (New York: Teachers' College Press).

—(2000) *The Market Approach to Education: An Analysis of America's First Voucher Program* (Princeton, NJ: Princeton University Press).

World Bank (2003) *World Development Report 2004: Making Services Work for Poor People* (Washington: World Bank).

# Afterword
Graham Haydon

*A reordering of fundamental political values is required.*

Howe, this volume, p. 88

Howe says this when questioning whether school choice can foster greater educational equality. It may well be that Howe would argue for a reordering of political values more generally; indeed that may be so for all three contributors, though they would not necessarily favour the *same* reordering (for instance, Howe and Tooley would certainly differ in how large a role they see for the state). The contributors have stuck to their brief here in focusing on education. In this afterword, as in the introduction, I want to broaden the scope a little, raising further questions about the notion of meritocracy, and about the role to be given to concern for the least advantaged.

## Meritocracy revisited

As noted in the Introduction, the Panel on Fair Access to the Professions (a Panel set up by a Prime Minister of a party that used to be considered left-wing in the British context, and probably would still be considered left-wing in American terms) says quite straightforwardly 'we want to see a meritocracy where individuals are able to advance on the basis of their talent and effort.' One might wonder whether there is much room for dispute about that; at any rate, if individuals are going to advance it may seem obviously fairer that they should do so on the basis of their talent and effort rather than because they happen to be born to parents who are wealthy, or of a particular social class, or particular ethnicity, and so on. The shared assumption in the background is that we are talking about a society in which it is taken for granted that some individuals advance beyond others in competition with those others. This is an explicit part of Brighouse's justification for being concerned about educational equality in the first place:

> The intuitive case for educational equality rests on an intuition about what it takes for a competition to be fair. . . . Modern industrial societies are structured so that socially produced rewards . . . are distributed unequally. Education is a crucial gateway to these rewards . . . It is unfair, then, if some get a worse education than others because, through no fault of their own, this puts them at a disadvantage in the competition for these unequally distributed goods. (Brighouse, this volume, p. 27)

Meritocracy, then, on this reading – as well as the 'Radical Conception' of equality that Brighouse also considers – is all about fairness to individuals, and accordingly it is often seen as obviously desirable. The Panel on Fair Access to the Professions acknowledges (briefly) that the idea has had its critics, including the person who first introduced the idea: 'It was Michael Young who first coined the term "meritocracy" in his 1958 book *Rise of the Meritocracy*, which warned of the consequences for a society in which the able progressed but the less able languished' (Panel on Fair Access to the Professions, Full Report, p. 27). This comment largely misses Young's point by ignoring the question of what it is that the able are progressing towards.

In Young's book it is quite clear that the hybrid Latin/Greek notion of meritocracy is formed by deliberate analogy with its genuine Greek predecessors 'democracy' and 'aristocracy'. All three refer to forms of society, distinguished by who it is that holds and exercises power (the second element in each word). Accordingly, a meritocracy is not just a set of educational arrangements that try to proportion the education each individual gets to their merit; it is a *kind of society* 'in which power and responsibility [are] as much proportioned to merit as education' (Young, 1961, p. 114). The central point of Young's satire (or dystopia) is that power and responsibility are exercised, not by an hereditary elite class, as in aristocracy, or by the people as (in theory at any rate) in democracy, but by those who have merit. Merit is defined initially as the sum of intelligence and effort (very like the combination of talent and effort that figures in recent conceptions of meritocracy) but in Young's future, as imagined in 1958, it is simply intelligence, as measured by sophisticated I.Q. tests, that comes to be dominant. In the real world five decades on, though I.Q. testing as such is less in favour, it is still progression up the educational ladder, certificated through testing and examination, that gets people into positions of status, responsibility and hence power.

Perhaps it seems right that those who are most intelligent should be the ones who exercise power. We should be mindful, though, of two things, both brought out in Young's book. First, intelligence is by no means the only quality that matters in the exercise of power and responsibility. Aristotle has a distinction between practical wisdom, which is an ethically positive quality, and cleverness, which is ethically neutral; intelligence seems to align with Aristotle's cleverness. Second, Young predicts that as those who ascend the educational ladder most successfully will support their own children and their cultural peers in doing the same, a new social class will begin to form.

Indeed, returning to the theme in 2001, Young wrote that the problem is not about the matching between individuals' ability and the jobs that they are doing; it is that 'those who are judged to have merit of a particular kind harden into a new social class without room in it for others' (Young, 2001). The evidence presented by the Panel on Fair Access to the Professions, showing many professions increasingly recruiting entrants from professional backgrounds, seems to go some way to support Young's claim.

It is, then, ironic that a shift in the way the term 'meritocratic' is understood has enabled the pursuit of meritocracy to be seen as the very way in which the evils of meritocracy, as Young saw it, can be avoided. The point of the meritocratic conception of equal opportunity, as outlined by Brighouse, is that the prospects of an individual should depend *solely* on her own talents and efforts independently of any advantages she may gain from, say, having professional parents. Yet, as we can see from the arguments over parental partiality that James Tooley raises in response to Harry Brighouse and Adam Swift, this very attempt to concentrate on the individual will, if our thinking is too simplistic, lead to an abstraction from the wider environmental and cultural factors that in reality will inevitably have their influence.

On the meritocratic conception of equal opportunity, there is one underlying value that matters most of all, and it is *not* equality. It is fairness (to individuals), as can be seen in the quotation from Brighouse above. Nevertheless, Brighouse does think that equality in education is one value that matters, but only alongside, and in some circumstances to be overridden by, family values and the good of the least advantaged. Both Howe and Tooley take some issue with Brighouse on the interpretation of these values and the priorities to be accorded to them. Tooley thinks that, if Brighouse is to hold on to his family values and his concern for the least advantaged, he should drop any distinct concern with equality altogether. Is that the right way to go in 'a re-ordering of fundamental political values'? Or is there some alternative reordering that would keep a distinctive place for equality as a value? In what follows I want to suggest – I use that word deliberately, for the amount of argument possible here is limited – that equality can have a distinct role. My limited argument will have three steps: to draw attention to the way that values can actually operate in people's motivation; to make some observations about concern for the least advantaged as a motivating value; to suggest that equality as a motivating value is significantly different from, and could be preferable to, concern for the least advantaged.

## Values as motivating factors in individual behaviour

I am sure the contributors to this volume do not dispute that values do not operate only in philosophical arguments nor only in government policies. They operate also in the thinking and the decisions made by individuals about their own lives, and by parents about the lives of their children.

The meritocratic conception of educational equality – and more especially, the discussion of school choice as a possible instrument of the meritocratic conception – tends to assume that parents are motivated primarily by the wish that the child should have the best possible education. This is inherently a competitive wish, since it cannot be that every child will have the best education. Perhaps it is not a strict truth of logic that it is impossible for every child to have the best education, since we might be able to imagine a world in which, somehow, it is possible for every child to get just exactly the sort of education that is best for that individual child. But clearly the world we live in is not like that. We assume both that the kind of education that is good for one child is good for another (at least across some central aspects of education), and that it is not realistically possible for the education of every child, in every school, to be equally good. So the motivation assumed on the meritocratic model inherently involves a wish that one's own child will do better than some other children will.

This inherently competitive motivation is not much softened if we say, with Brighouse (this volume, p. 57) that the information parents need is not how good a school is, but how high the probability is that it will be good for one's own child. For the culture (especially in Britain) of a quasi-market in schooling backed up by league tables encourages the idea that certain schools are good for most, if not all, of the children attending them, while other schools are rather poor for most, if not all, of the children attending them.

Interestingly, it was the 'semi-skilled' choosers in the Gewirtz, Ball and Bowe study (reported by Brighouse, this volume, pp. 22–3) who thought more of finding the 'good' school rather than the right one for their child. We might wonder whether this is such a bad basis for choice. It is only from a certain perspective that the focus on the right school for one's child as the crucial factor is *the* right way to choose; to want one's own child together with other children from the neighbourhood to attend a school that is good for all of them is a significantly different consideration, and is a consideration that parents can – and at least some parents do – take into account.

If the meritocratic assumptions about parental motivation are right, there will be no place in parental motivation for either equality *or* a concern for the benefit of the least advantaged. These will be values that enter into schooling and its outcomes *only* at the level of policy; roughly, it will be the business of government to try to design institutions in such a way that, while parents pursue only the good of their own children, the system as a whole works in a way that is not too bad from the point of view of equality, or not too bad for those who are worst off, or both. It is not surprising that such a system is hard to design.

Yet it *is* possible for parents, like any other citizens – or rather, like citizens under any other description – to be motivated by more than a concern that their own child should do as well as possible. It *is* possible for citizens who are parents to care about equality and to care about the fate of the least advantaged in their society. It is even possible for such values to be quite widely acknowledged, not just as requirements on government policy, but within a culture.

Consider an example that comes up in Tooley's dispute with Brighouse and Swift about legitimate parental partiality: taking one's children on exotic holidays. It is a little odd that Tooley mentions this in the same breath as reading bedtime stories to one's children, since the two cases are very different. Reading bedtime stories to one's child is something that virtually any parent can do, or at least any parent in a society that succeeds in achieving full adult literacy and that is humane enough to enable people to have access to books without having to purchase them (e.g. through free public lending libraries). Taking children on exotic holidays is an option that is much more restricted in terms of parents' income and no doubt in terms of the mores of the parents' cultural reference group. Some parents will be able and willing to take their children on exotic holidays; of these parents, some at least may be sensible of their relatively privileged position in their society and may think it a pity that such holidays are not available to more children.

Now consider the following imagined scenario. There is a voluntary organization that exists to make exotic holidays possible for children who would otherwise not have the opportunity to go on such holidays. This organization suggests that any parents taking their own children on an exotic holiday should make a voluntary donation (say of 10 per cent of the cost of their holiday with their own children) towards the fund for holidays for the under-privileged children. There would be no coercion, no interference with parental freedom, in this scheme. It is possible – I am making no claims about its being likely, starting from where we are now – it is possible that supporting this scheme could become part of the cultural values of the society. Parents who are able to take their children on exotic holidays could come to be just a little ashamed about doing so without contributing something to make such holidays possible for others.

I shall only mention and say nothing further here about the complication that such parents might also think they should be limiting their own exotic travel for the sake of the environment. That complication actually supports my overall point here: that we should not simply assume that parents will always, or should always, do what they consider to be best for their own child, regardless of other considerations; citizens who are parents can be motivated in part by extra-familial values (some parents *are* concerned about the real world where 'millions of children are without any education at all' – Tooley, this volume, p. 105). These extra-familial values may include a concern for the least advantaged, and they may include equality. It is time to say a little more about these values.

## Revisiting the benefit of the least advantaged

What would be the likely motivation of the parents in the scenario just considered? Hardly equality, for we are not imagining them wanting all people to have an equal number of equally exotic holidays. Their concern seems much more likely to be a concern that the lives of those who are worst off should be made at least a little better.

The contributors to this volume have all commented on the difference between equality and the benefit of the least advantaged as factors influencing policy; I want now to comment on the difference between them in the motivation of individuals and groups. As often, a simplified example can help to make the point. So imagine again (as in my Rawlsian sketch in the Introduction) a new small society being set up by people who have no shared tradition of values to guide them, only perhaps a hope for a better life than they have been experiencing (there are historical examples of people founding societies intended to be utopias). These people recognize that individuals will have different skills and talents and that it may well happen that some people can achieve a better material quality of life than others. They are (let's suppose) not devoid of altruism. What values might develop in such a community?

One possibility is that those who turn out to be relatively well off will accept that the position of the worst off should be improved. Accordingly, the well off will take steps to see that the worst off are not *too* badly off (according to the judgement of the well off). Their motivation may be a moral and conscientious one. The motivation might, for instance, have been that of the landed aristocracy in eighteenth-century England who accepted a degree of responsibility for the welfare of their tenants, or of the (relatively rare) nineteenth-century philanthropic mill owners who built better than average housing for their workers. It might be the motivation too of middle-class parents now who are able and willing to get their children into better than average schools while trying conscientiously to take some political steps to see that schools attended by those less fortunate are at least not as bad as they might be.[1]

In fact as a motivation a concern for the benefit of the least advantaged fits rather well with the ethos of meritocracy. Those who can are to rise to the top in terms of influence and responsibility; they are to use their influence, responsibly, to help those who do not have the same natural advantages. (Remember that at the moment I am considering, not the effects of this or that policy, but possible motivations at a more personal and cultural level.) It is perhaps a reason for caution about this meritocratic attitude that it may have an analogy on the global level, to which Tooley rightly draws our attention. Do the stances sometimes taken in the developed world towards the still developing, often post-colonial world, sometimes amount to the idea: 'we – the developed Western countries – have succeeded through our talent and effort; now we will help to improve your position.'? It hardly needs saying that this is not a stance of equality between nations.

## The voice of equality in the conversation of citizens

It is clear that there is not necessarily anything remotely egalitarian about the motivation of the well off who help, and may even accept they have an obligation to help, the worst off. In my simplified scenario of the new society, in its first version, what happened was that a culture developed in which the better off and the worst off in some respects did *not* share the same values. Both the worst off and the already well off may have the desire that their own lot should be improved – that much at least is shared – but a sense of obligation to improve the lot of the worst off is not a motivation that can be shared by the worst off themselves. There was, however, another way in which the value culture of the small society could have developed. It might have developed as a community sharing the understanding that all its members are in the same boat and that the resources developed within the community are resources to be used for the benefit of the community. With this understanding can go the sense, not that a part of the community ought to accept some responsibility for another part, but that all have a shared responsibility for all.

Put like that, this idea of a shared sense of responsibility may sound hopelessly vague, or unrealistically utopian, or dangerously socialist (for readers for whom 'socialist' is a pejorative term). I am actually not trying here to *advocate* a certain social motivation, for that would need more argument than there is space for. My point here is to draw attention to what we might call (borrowing the form of the phrase, if nothing else, from Oakeshott) the voice of equality in the conversation of citizens, a voice that can influence both their own behaviour and public policy.

The voice of equality expresses a different motivation, a different underlying value orientation, from, simply, concern for the benefit of the least advantaged. This qualitative difference in the underlying value orientation remains *even if* it is true that basing public policy on a concern for the least advantaged would do more to improve the lot of the least advantaged than would an egalitarian public policy. It is possible to put positive value on the orientation expressed in the voice of equality independently of a comparison of the effects of putting one or the other into practice.

This voice is perhaps little heard now.[2] It was easier to speak in this voice when terms such as 'fraternity' and 'solidarity' still had resonance, and when the notion of socialism could be used without embarrassment or apology. It was once heard, I would suggest, in the thinking about public policy that led in Britain to the formation of the National Health Service and later, to support for a system of comprehensive schools. It was heard earlier in the USA in the writings of John Dewey. It can be expressed in a more collective version of the self-help to which Tooley refers (this volume, pp. 120–1). It is still sometimes heard in the thinking of parents who make a conscious choice *not* to pursue by all means available the schooling that will be optimum for their child, but rather to support their local school, even if it not yet the best, because they think they can help to make it better and that their child will thereby benefit along with others. While this voice will certainly agree that where competition is inevitable (in appointment to jobs, for instance), it must be fair, it will also prefer to see a less competitive society in areas where that is possible; and it will believe that in education it *is* possible. While it will accept that Brighouse's 'radical' conception of education is radical against a background of meritocracy, it will suggest that there could be a more thoroughly radical conception that would not begin by putting individual competition centre-stage.

It is not my argument here that everything said in this voice is realistic or that it could be the sole basis for good policy. My modest conclusion is that the silence of this voice would be an impoverishment of the ethical environment in which public debate, not least that about educational equality, goes on.

## Notes

1. See Adam Swift's *How Not To Be a Hypocrite: School Choice for the Morally Perplexed Parent* (2003) for discussion of the rights and wrongs of this and related parental positions.

2. For a recent expression of this voice see Fielding, M., 'On the Necessity of Radical State Education: Democracy and the Common School' (2008).

## References

Fielding, M. (2008) 'On the Necessity of Radical State Education: Democracy and the Common School', in Halstead, M. and Haydon, G. (eds) *The Common School and the Comprehensive Ideal* (Oxford: Wiley-Blackwell).

Swift, A. (2003) *How Not To Be a Hypocrite: School Choice for the Morally Perplexed Parent* (London: Routledge).

*Unleashing Aspiration: The Final Report of the Panel on Fair Access to the Professions* July 2009, at http://www.cabinetoffice.gov.uk/media/227102/fair-access.pdf (accessed on 21 November 2009).

Young, M. (1961) *The Rise of the Meritocracy 1870–2033* (Harmondsworth: Penguin) [First published Thames & Hudson 1958].

—(2001) 'Down with Meritocracy', in *The Guardian* (London) 29 June 2001.

# Index